faith
step by step

for **Aafje**

Other books in English by Reinder Bruinsma:

The Day God Created
It's Time
Matters of Life and Death
Our Awesome God

First published in 2006
Copyright © 2006
All rights reserved. No part of this publication
may be reproduced in any form without
prior permission from the publisher.
British Library Cataloguing in Publication Data.
A catalogue record for this book is available
from the British Library.

ISBN 1-904685-26-9

Cover picture © Comstock images/alamy

Published by The Stanborough Press Ltd
Grantham, England.

Printed in Thailand

faith

step by step
finding God and yourself

Reinder Bruinsma

About the Author

Reinder Bruinsma was born in 1942 in the Netherlands and has worked in various parts of the world, in the service of the Seventh-day Adventist Church. He has worked as pastor, editor, teacher and church administrator. His overseas mission experience was in West Africa (1984-1991). Subsequently he was connected with the Mission Institute of the SDA Church (on the campus of Andrews University (MI, USA; 1991-1994). He then moved to the United Kingdom and was soon afterwards elected as the executive secretary of one of the European regions of the SDA Church (1995-2001). He currently serves as the president of the Adventist Church in the Netherlands.

After having earned a BA at Newbold College/Andrews University (1965), he earned an MA (1966) at Andrews University. In 1972 he was awarded the BD-Honour degree and the PhD degree (1993) from the University of London.

Dr Bruinsma is the author of numerous scholarly and popular articles and of seventeen books in Dutch and English, some of which have been translated into other languages.

Acknowledgements

Dr Jan Paulsen and Dr Bertil Wiklander for their encouragement with regard to this project and for having taken time in their busy schedules to read the manuscript and provide helpful comments. I would also like to express appreciation for the constructive criticism of others, most notably: Mr Lee Gallagher and Dr David Marshall at the Stanborough Press, and Mr A. C. Balk, who critiqued the book from an informed 'layman's' perspective. As always, my wife has tried to convince me to reduce the number of technical terms that I tend to use and has saved me from many embarrassing grammatical and stylistic errors, so that I could provide a reasonably clean text to the editor at the Stanborough Press.

All Bible texts are taken from the New International Version

Contents

Introduction	**7**
A momentous shift	8
Are you postmodern?	9
A discovery in ten steps	11

one
Meaning	**16**
Different answers to a perplexing question	17
Inside out	20
Or outside in?	23
Explaining the origin of life	26
The fine tuning of the universe	27
The eye	28
Enough proof?	29

two
Truth	**33**
How did Truth become truths?	34
Can we still hope to find Truth?	37
Truth about God	42
Divine communication?	44
An extraordinary book	46
Believing truth	50

three
Faith	**51**
How normal is faith?	52
Faith is normal	54
How to get faith if you want it	57
The 'stuff' of belief	63

four
Hope	**67**
Hopelessness versus hope	68
The basis of hope	72
Hope for each individual	77
The mystery of death and beyond	80
Hope for the world	83

five Grace — 87
- The mystery of evil — 88
- The even greater mystery — 91
- Sin and guilt: what are we talking about? — 92
- Dealing with the problem of sin and evil — 95
- The Himalaya of God's grace — 99
- Forgiveness — 106

six Rest — 108
- We need rest — 109
- Time set aside — 113
- How do we rest? — 117
- What or when? — 121

seven Community — 124
- Alone or together? — 125
- The ultimate support group — 127
- What does the word 'church' mean? — 129
- Rituals — 134
- But do we really need to join? — 137
- Which church? — 139

eight Responsibility — 142
- Caretakers of God's creation — 144
- Stewards of our body — 148
- Christian time management — 151
- A philosophy of sharing — 154

nine Commitment — 160
- Servants — 163
- Slavery or freedom? — 169
- Making the most of our gifts — 171
- Discipline — 172
- Fully committed — 175

ten Mission — 177

References — 183

Introduction

Over the last few decades I have written a number of books, some in English and some in Dutch, my native tongue. Some have been translated into a few other languages. So it should not come as a surprise that I once again get behind my laptop and try my hand at a new book. This time also it will be a book about faith, and once again I shall write from a particular Christian perspective. But this book is going to be radically different from anything I have written previously. Why? Because of a number of changes that have taken place.

In the first place I myself have changed. Even though I still believe in most of the *things* I believed in some twenty-five years ago, I have changed significantly *in the way* in which I believe. Some things have become more important to me, while other things have somewhat receded into the background. But, more importantly, I tend to ask much more *why* I believe what I believe and *what difference it makes* that I believe what I believe, than simply to be satisfied with the confidence that the things I believe in are true.

But I am not the only one who has changed. The world in which I live has also changed dramatically. And with it the people around me. So this must be a different kind of book if I am to have any hope of communicating meaningfully with my readers. Without exaggeration, it can be stated that the world – the Western world at any rate – has moved into a new era. Or to use a term that has become part of the lingo of today: *modernity* has given way to *postmodernity*. My goal in this book will be to talk specifically to people who have travelled a considerable distance along the path from modern to postmodern.

When did this shift from modernity to postmodernity take place? It is, of course, impossible to pinpoint the beginning and the end of any era in a precise manner. It was not immediately clear to those who lived in the fifteenth and sixteenth centuries that the period of the 'Middle Ages' was coming to its end and that the 'modern' age had begun. It is only from the perspective of history that we now have a reasonably clear picture of that gradual transition. Likewise, the full picture of what is now happening to our world will only gradually become clear. But that something is indeed happening and that the world is in transition is beyond any doubt.

A momentous shift

When we use the word 'modern' or a related term to refer to the period which followed the Middle Ages, we do so in a particular way and not as the opposite for the term 'old-fashioned'. Modernity is a label for what has also been called the *Enlightenment Project*, which got under way when people were leaving the Middle Ages behind them and beginning to think differently. From the early seventeenth century onwards, the philosophical approach of the famous French thinker René Descartes (1596-1650) began to sink in. His famous dictum *Cogito Ergo Sum* (I think, therefore I am) became the foundation for a new way of looking at man and God. Autonomous man, endowed with reason, and soon also fortified by the new scientific method which was developed by men like Francis Bacon (1561-1626) and Isaac Newton (1642-1727), became the measure of all things. Man was going to solve the world's problems. God was increasingly situated at a distance, while the recently discovered laws of nature kept the universe ticking over in an orderly manner. The future would be marked by continuous progress, as the enormous resources of this planet were exploited for man's benefit.

Towards the end of the nineteenth century and in the early twentieth century, this approach to life was beginning to run out of steam, as Friedrich Nietschze (1844-1900), Sigmund Freud (1856-1939) and other radical thinkers came on the scene. New philosophical approaches which focused on language and the interpretation of texts began to blossom, and delivered a message of relativism, uncertainty, and even pessimism, which found fertile soil in the minds of many twentieth-century hearers. The Holocaust of the mid-twentieth century, if anything, made it impossible to think of life as it had been.

Philosophers in Europe and also in the United States began to emphasize that the time of the 'grand narratives' such as Marxism, Communism and Christianity had eclipsed. There were, they said, no all-encompassing systems of thought which offer a comprehensive explanation of life; there were only fragmented, and often contradictory, 'smaller stories' of individuals and groups in all their diversity. '*All is difference*', they proclaimed. 'And all judgement needs to be *deferred*! There are no absolutes; *Truth* has been replaced by *truths*.' From the 1970s onwards the terms *postmodernism* and *postmodernity* came into use to describe the changes that became more and more apparent in the arts and in architecture, and then also in philosophy and even theology. Today the term has become a catch-all label that can be attached to almost anything. But though, admittedly, the term is imprecise and postmodernity means different things to different people, it cannot be denied that something is going on, particularly in the Western world. The Enlightenment era has come, or is rapidly coming, to an end, and we participate, whether we want to or not, in an unprecedented process of change.

Are you postmodern?

Before we go any further, let us look at what a postmodern person is. What does she think? What does he do? Where is he most likely to be found? There is no shortage of recent books which list the main characteristics of the postmodern man and woman. Most authors will indicate that there is a superficial kind of postmodernism, which is, at least to some extent, synonymous with consumerism and a shallow pursuit of pleasure, and which allows its adherents to live most of their lives in a virtual world. But there is more to postmodernity than that, and in most cases this superficial description of postmodernism would be unfair. Rather than describing the average postmodern person as an amusement-seeking, gadget-happy, one-dimensional individual, metaphors like *nomad, zapper* or *stroller* might be more apt. And it should also be said that there is often an interesting mix of modernity and postmodernity in one and the same person.

Here are some of the recognised values and ideals of postmodern thinking. If these thought processes seem in alignment with your own (and remember they are only basic guides), then it is quite likely you have a postmodern approach to life.

- The idea of progress is largely abandoned. The postmodern person no longer believes that everything will become better and better. Science is not the unconditional blessing it was once thought to be.
- There are no absolutes. We all have our own private truths. Communities and cultures have their own 'language' games. What they talk about and believe in does not necessarily relate to any objective reality. Everything is subjective, relative, uncertain, preliminary, and ambiguous.
- The metanarratives (grand stories) and the grand ideals of the past have disappeared. We must be content with more limited, partial explanations, which will need constant revision.
- Postmodern people like combining incompatible elements. In the arts we find a great interest in collation, a mixing of artistic styles, a blurring of the lines between real life and fiction, between the real and the virtual.
- Scientists are becoming more modest in their claims. They confess that they often tend to see what they want to see, and that many of the so-called foundations of science may not be so certain after all.
- People realize more and more that they live in a global village. The computer – the symbol of postmodernity *par excellence* – gives them instant access to the world. Yet at the same time global strategies and alliances are under suspicion, and there is a growing interest in regional and local issues.
- The postmodern person has a strong dislike for religious institutions, but is open to spirituality. In fact, some advocate the need for a re-enchantment of the world. Mystery is OK. The non-rational, New Age-type approach to the questions of life is popular. The emphasis has shifted from religious *truth* that is codified in doctrine to religious *experience*.

Once you are aware of the main characteristics of the postmodern mindset, you see the impact of postmodern thinking everywhere – *in yourself and the people you work and live with, and also in the world around you.*

Look at some recent buildings in western cities; no longer the 'modern' box-like monotonous structures of concrete, steel and glass. Ornamentation is back and styles from different periods are combined, so that postmodern building can tell its own story rather than the standard 'modern' story of power, order and efficiency. You will easily detect the postmodern trends in many recent novels which blend stories from different periods and mix real life with the world of fantasy; in films which leave you wondering where the historical ends and the fictional begins; and in the 'info-tainment' and 'docu-soaps' on television. You find the ambiguity in the political arena, as, for instance, in parts of Europe, where a majority of the people support the idea of European unity, but at the same time will do almost anything do protect their local culture and especially their local dialect.

One quickly detects the postmodern approach of many 'western' people to religion and to the church. Religion is 'in', but the institutional church is totally 'out'. Experience and emotion are OK, but doctrinal small print is considered mostly irrelevant. Absolute, propositional truth is largely replaced by 'what works for me', and many Bible scholars claim there are as many legitimate ways to interpret the Bible as there are readers. Christianity has become one religious option among a series of world religions – all are considered equally valid, historically and culturally conditioned, responses of the human self to the Beyond!

A discovery in ten steps

Let me be totally upfront. This book will be about religion and faith, and it will approach things from a particular Christian perspective. I do not want to leave any doubt about this, for if there is one thing that you, as postmodern readers, want, it is total honesty, integrity and transparency. You do not want to be duped somewhere along the way. So, if this is not your cup of tea, you have been duly warned, and this will be the moment to put the book aside. I hope, however, that you will allow me to develop my thoughts in favour of the Christian faith and that you will join me on this journey of discovery.

I have divided our pilgrimage into ten consecutive steps, or chapters, each of them taking us a step further along the path of discovery. In the first chapter I talk about the question of meaning. Is there a deeper meaning in the history of mankind and in our personal story? If so, where and how do we find this? I suggest that the concept of meaning is tied to the question as to whether there is a Something or Someone we may call 'God'. If God exists, we may wonder how we can relate to him or her[1] (chapter two). If he does indeed exist, we would have certain expectations of what he is like and of what he does. Are there things we can know about him for certain? Or are we just left to our own imaginations, and is it really anyone's guess what God is like? Traditionally, Christians have believed that the Bible provides reliable (and supernatural) information on this topic. Is it still possible to believe this, or is the Bible merely a record of how Jewish and Christian beliefs have developed and how people in a rather distant past have experienced their beliefs?

If, as I have come to believe, we can know certain things about God and if, indeed, we can find reliable information about him in the Bible, we can take the next step (chapter three). Knowing *about* God is little more than satisfying our intellectual capacities. *Knowing* God by establishing some kind of relationship with him goes far beyond just knowing something about him and gives existential meaning to the conviction that God exists. Trust and faith are key issues that arise in this context.

Related to this is the concept of hope (chapter four). If we can meaningfully relate to a God who is somehow responsible for all that is and happens, the world (all of us included) is not left to its own devices. This provides a supernatural context to the history of mankind and to our own personal history. Although many aspects of life may remain mysterious, there would appear to be a distinct frame of reference which provides direction and hope.

Having ventured these four fundamental steps together, we shall proceed with five further inalienable elements of the Christian faith. If we come to the point where we accept that there is a God who is behind everything that exists, we shall be faced with an enormous dilemma. 'God' cannot be God if he is not fundamentally good. Yet there are so many things in this world, and in our own lives, which are clearly wrong. They leave us sad, dissatisfied and discouraged. There is sickness and death, war and hunger, poverty and hatred. How do we account for this? I have to be honest; this is a question I shall not be able to answer in a fully satisfactory manner. The existence of 'evil' has always been an immense dilemma which has turned many people away from the Christian faith. For how can a loving God, who is alleged to be all-wise and all-powerful, allow the terrible things we see around us? This is a particularly difficult issue for postmodern people. Chapter five will probe this problem and will, I hope, challenge you to consider the options with an open mind. I shall share my deep belief that God has provided for a remedy that is bigger than anything I, or anyone else, can bring to the table. He has opened a way towards restoration. Admittedly, it will take a further leap of faith to accept this.

Then (in chapter six) we shall touch on a very practical element that is part and parcel of that restoration. Christianity is not escapist in the sense that it tells its adherents to retreat from real life and from everyday responsibilities. But, on the other hand, there is a provision for charging our batteries and finding true rest and genuine depth on a regular basis. It can, I suggest, be the perfect antidote for our life of stress, with its constant threat of burn-out and chronic fatigue. If there is a relevant feature in the lifestyle which is informed by Christian principles, it is the weekly day of rest with everything it implies. When we have come this far, I hope the reader will also be willing to consider (chapter seven) my belief that there is great value in joining others who have also come to have faith in God. There is great joy, and it builds inner strength, in being together with others who have entered into a relationship with God.

This community of believers is more than the sum total of the individuals that are part of it, as it is also (chapter eight) intimately connected with the concept of relating meaningfully to the world around us. If God is indeed the Designer and ultimate Maker of everything there is, we shall show appreciation for that astounding fact by looking after this world, and after our personal resources, in a responsible way.

In the end, it all boils down to making some clear decisions about how we want to live in view of the convictions that give structure to our inner life (chapter nine). However, it seems that postmodern people tend to shy away from making ultimate commitments. I notice that many have a deep-rooted tendency to keep their options open and to stop short of total involvement. They apparently hate to burn any of those bridges that allow for a last-minute escape. I must admit that I have discovered this inclination at times in myself. Yet if the Christian faith is what it claims to be there can, I believe, be no other valid response than a one hundred per cent 'yes'. There can be no question of a prolonged 'wait and see', of a provisional acceptance or a divided loyalty.

Christianity is about Christ. It claims that the Christian God became visible in the unique person of Jesus Christ. Being a Christian is not, primarily, consenting to a number of theoretical statements about God and what he did through Jesus Christ, but it is, first of all, a relationship, a way of life, a commitment to ideals. It is a commitment to a Person to whom we owe our total allegiance. This may all sound rather other-worldly or even strange, but, remember: this is stage nine, almost at the end of our journey of discovery together. You will better appreciate what I mean when you have followed me up to that point.

Chapter ten adds one final step. When we have come this far and have, hopefully, discovered the most amazing relationship of our lives, we shall want to share what we have found. After all, who really wants to keep a good thing totally to himself?

For many readers this is probably not going to be a comfortable book. Some people in my own church may feel uneasy with some of the language I use. They may miss some familiar themes, and may wonder why I seem to take some considerable detours when things appear to be so straightforward (to them). Well, this book is not written for them. There are plenty of books in which they will find all the minutiae of their beliefs in a form they enjoy. I am, however, writing primarily for those who are at the fringes of the church, or do not belong to my church or to any other church.

This book will not be complicated reading because of a multitude of philosophical or theological concepts which require a lot of technical knowledge in these areas. But, though I try hard to keep it relatively simple in vocabulary, and there will be only the occasional footnote, this does not mean that it will be simplistic. At least that is my intention. It will not be easy in the sense that it will require a response from those who decide to embark on this ten-stage journey as a personal discovery project. There may even be some risk. Some thoughts may be unsettling, and, as we go along, the book may raise issues that will refuse to go away. It will be impossible to remain neutral. For in the end, when a person confronts the One who is the personification of Christianity, he will have to say 'yes' or 'no'. Again, let me be upfront about my agenda: I hope this book will help at least some readers to see how wonderful it can be to have a relationship with an awesome, loving God.

Chapter one

Meaning

Have you never wondered about the meaning of life? When you see the images of horror, cruelty and pain flashing across your television screen? When you hear the stories of people who seem to be the target of every imaginable form of misfortune and suffering? When you visit a hospital ward where children with terminal diseases spend the few remaining weeks or months of their short lives?

Isn't this the great question that keeps coming back: Is life worth living? Is there meaning to life? To life in general? To my life? What can possibly be the meaning of the short period of misery of the millions of children who die from neglect or from poverty, hunger or thirst? What meaning can be there be to the lives of those who are born with a severe mental or physical handicap and have to be cared for in specialized institutions? What meaning does life have for those who eke out a minimal existence on the garbage heaps of Cairo or Mexico City? And what meaning can there be for the millions of women who are routinely abused and are denied the freedom even to move a few yards outside of their homes? What meaning does life have for those whose existence consists of lots of hard and tedious work, very little sleep and not much else?

We are conceived and born without our permission. Our average life expectancy is less than a hundred years. Of one thing, however, we can be absolutely sure: one day we shall die. For many who have already died there was little joy in what they experienced between the beginning and the end of their existence.

The quest for meaning is just as urgent for those who live reasonably sheltered lives in the Western world. Many who have a solid bank account, a secure job and a comfortable two-and-a-half bathroom home with a double garage wonder whether that is all there is to life. What do you get out of life if it is just work and recreation? What is the real satisfaction one gets out of life after one has tried everything there is to try, and one has been there, seen that, done that, etc.? Even when you have the money to buy anything you fancy, there may well come a moment when you wonder why you should bother with acquiring more things than you actually need. Of course, many will argue that the meaning of life is not just linked to material things. They realize that life is also relationships: a partner, children, friends and neighbours. But, let's face it: So many relationships deteriorate and end in acrimonious dispute. So many promising marriages and longstanding friendships turn sour. So many children give their parents nothing but heartache and trouble. So many people end their years in utter loneliness and cry in despair that their lives have lost all real meaning.

No wonder that Albert Camus, the famous French novelist and playwright (1913-1960), once wrote, 'There is but one truly serious philosophical problem, and that is suicide. Judging whether life is or is not worth living amounts to answering the fundamental question of philosophy. All the rest . . . these are games . . . .'[2]

Different answers to a perplexing question

The question of meaning extends far beyond our individual lives. Why is there life on this planet (and possibly elsewhere in the universe)? Did it just evolve through a long chain of accidents, or out of necessity, with no real purpose? Is there meaning in history, in the rise and fall of world empires, in the history of the nation of which we happen to be a part?

One answer to the question about meaning is straightforward. Many will say: There is no meaning to life, no overarching purpose. There simply is no moral framework which may guide us as to what is right or wrong. And, indeed, without a standard on which to build a system of morality (God, law, ideals of freedom, justice, etc.), any decision as to what is right or wrong would seem arbitrary. Your guess would be as good as mine. We are here, but shall never know why we are here, and we are going nowhere. This school of thought is called *nihilism*. The Latin root for the word is *nihil*, which means *nothing*. It aptly describes what it offers: absolutely zilch. It leaves us empty-handed. Concepts like love, justice, solidarity and joy remain empty shells, and any setback in daily life may cause a person to wonder why she should bother to continue living at all. We are back to the distressing statement of Albert Camus!

Some try to be practical. They believe there is nothing 'higher' – nothing beyond what we can experience – but sense that we have little choice but to make the best of our predicament. So, it will help, they suggest, if we establish a few norms that will order our society and will make life somewhat more bearable. One such approach, which over time has been particularly popular in the United States, maintains that we should try to aim for the greatest amount of pleasure and satisfaction for the greatest possible number of people. This school of thought is called *utilitarianism*. We must accept the inevitable. Not everybody will be happy and will be able to live a fulfilled life. There are all kinds of things that just seem to work against us, but we can at least try to exercise damage control and pragmatically agree to do the best we can for as many people as possible.

Others again have suggested a totally different response to the question of meaning. They argue that life has meaning because it must exist for a reason. Everything that is has a cause. We see this basic rule confirmed all around us. It is the underlying common-sense principle on which we operate. The fact that I lie on the street waiting for an ambulance is caused by the fact that I was knocked down by a car. This accident was caused by the fact that the driver was inattentive. He was inattentive because he was thinking about the difficult meeting he was going to have in the office, which was caused by the dip in the sales through his part of the organization, which was caused by increased competition from abroad, which was caused . . . etc., etc.

Thus, every cause is related to some prior cause, and at the beginning of the long chain of causes there must be a *First Cause,* which has traditionally been called 'God'. Thus God is the Fundamental Cause of all that is. He is somehow responsible for the fact that there are things, large and small, from the gigantic universe, of which we can see only a small part, to the microbes that are invisible to the naked eye.

It is because there is a God, these people say, that there is also a moral order. For a God who is at the beginning of everything may be expected to establish a fundamental norm for what is 'good' and what violates this 'goodness'. It would also imply that the human individual is not here by mere chance, but that his existence is part of some divine plan. His existence is not a strange coincidence but somehow has meaning in the overall scheme of things.

To many, it seems an attractive option to look for the meaning of life in a solution which assigns the key role to a 'God' who is the First Cause, and who by his very existence provides a framework of meaning. It is my belief – which I shall put to you for your consideration – that the hypothesis that there is a God who is ultimately responsible for what exists and happens in the world and in the universe is at least as credible as the miserable idea that there is no organizing principle whatsoever behind everything that is, and no moral framework which may direct the way in which we live.

Granted, it is a *hypothesis* which leaves many questions unanswered. One of the issues which will always raise its dubious head is why so many things do not seem to work as we think they should, in the universe, on this planet and in our individual lives. Is this hypothetical 'God' – as we would expect a God to be – really successful in what he undertakes? Or are we dealing with a God who has left plenty of loose ends and, unfortunately, has not been able to harness the forces of nature in such a way that floods in Bangladesh, terrible droughts in sub-Saharan Africa, and devastating tsunamis in Southeast Asia are avoided? How can we possibly believe in a God who created us not only with mortal bodies, but allowed some of us to be born with serious construction defects, and failed to make the cells of our bodies immune to leukaemia and a host of other cancers? In a God who has an eye for beauty, as is evident from the many gorgeous things we see around us, but also allows for a horrific amount of cruelty in nature, and for terrible waste?

Yet, in spite of the many questions we may have, I suggest that the hypothesis that there is a God is appealing and deserves our thoughtful attention. If there is a God, this would explain many things, and we would have a starting point for our journey of discovery. It would go a long way towards finding some basic meaning for our lives. If we could be reasonably sure that there is a Something or Someone we would call 'God', we would then, of course, try to find out as much as we could about this God.

But let us not run ahead of ourselves. For the fact that the hypothesis that there is a God who can provide meaning to our existence is attractive does not automatically imply that it can be proven to be more than a hypothesis. After all, it may just be wishful thinking and pie in the sky.

Inside out

So, where do we go from here? Is there a way to 'prove' the existence of a God? Or, if that is not possible in any definitive sense, can we at least show that the God-hypothesis is not just a wild guess, but that, for the time being, it may be a credible point of departure or a 'justifiable' belief? I think we can. There are two lines of approach which we may follow as we try to increase our confidence that there is more 'out there'. The first is from the *inside out*, while the second is from the *outside in*.[3]

The first approach starts with ourselves, our own consciousness and our own feelings and inner, private, experiences, and will then attempt to draw some conclusions about a Reality which we assume to have caused those experiences. The second approach tells us to look first at the world around us, and then leads us to wonder what conclusions we may arrive at, if we look in the right way and in the right places. For many who have given a lot of thought to this, it appears to be a matter of either/or. We must, they say, opt for the inside-out approach or for the outside-in approach. However, I am not so sure that the choice is so clear cut and I tend to think that both approaches lead us to significant insights that may, in fact, reinforce each other. I hope you will give me the chance to explain.

The inside-out approach has become quite dominant in the last two centuries. It claims that thinking about God originates in our own inner self. Talking about something like an *inner self* involves, of course, the basic assumption that human beings are more than just matter, and that thinking and feeling and loving and hating, etc., cannot be reduced to mere chemical and physiological processes in our nervous system. It assumes that human beings have something that is intimately linked with their physical bodies but is in some way separate from them and is more than 'just' matter. Christians have usually referred to this 'something' as the *soul*. A more neutral term which will suffice for now is the concept of *mind*.

There are thinkers who deny that there is such a duality of matter and mind. They are referred to as *materialists*. But although there are many complicated issues involved in this discussion, I suggest that, for now, we assume that there is this distinction between the physical body and something else, and that what we call 'mind' or 'inner self' cannot be reduced to the material brain.

Human beings can think. They can compare notes and are able and often more than willing to argue. They can make more or less rational choices. But they also have emotions. They can love and hate. They can trust and mistrust, like and dislike. They can feel lonely and rejected, or totally at peace with the world and with others. They can enter into emotional relationships and can feel dependent, or in charge and responsible. Beyond these feelings, which can be described as personal or interpersonal, there is something far deeper, which is experienced by such a vast number of people that it suggests a special significance. Friedrich Schleiermacher (1768-1834), a famous German theologian who is still very influential, labelled this phenomenon as a 'feeling of absolute dependence'. We know deep down, he said, that there is Something on which we *ultimately depend*. By that he meant that there is a spiritual dimension in our existence which cannot be explained in material terms. Another way of saying this is that human beings appear to be 'incurably religious'. Interestingly enough, whenever and wherever vestiges of ancient civilizations are found, there is undeniable evidence of religious interest. And whenever and wherever, in more recent times, organized religion in its more traditional forms [the church] has been on the wane, other types of religiosity [New Age, belief in angels or spirits, Wicca, etc.] seem to emerge and even blossom.

Researchers have found a widespread sense of a *Something Beyond* among totally diverse cultures, and among peoples of all social classes and with a wide range of personalities and educational backgrounds. They have discovered this inexplicable awareness of a connection, a link with something beyond ourselves: *a feeling of ultimate and absolute dependence*.

How is this phenomenon to be explained? Are we justified in thinking that this feeling of ultimate dependence can best be explained by the fact that there *actually exists* a Something on which we feel dependent, or a Someone to whom we feel unmistakably drawn? That would, it seems to me (as it has done and does to many others), be a far more likely scenario than to assume that this sense of a Beyond has somehow originated spontaneously as part of a baffling evolutionary process during which *homo sapiens* developed, and has, like a virus, spread to millions of people in all times and of all cultures that descended from him.

Once we somehow sense the existence of a Beyond and have become more consciously aware of this feeling of ultimate dependence; and once we have decided that we may refer to this Someone on whom, or Something on which, we are ultimately dependent as 'God', we are free to start using our imagination about this God. We must admit that it may well be that anything we affirm about this alleged 'God' is just that: a figment of our imagination. It may just come from the 'inside', shaped by our own 'inner self'. If we cannot avoid the question, how can we test the objective truth of any claims we make about this 'God'? We will need to return to this issue. But first, hang in, and consider another important aspect.

Or outside in?

The second approach which I refer to as the *outside-in* approach suggests that we must take a close look at the world outside of us – the cosmos, this planet, nature, human and animal life – because there may be features that point to Something or Someone beyond what we can observe. This approach has a long history. It has had its supporters throughout the history of Christianity, but has met with heavy criticism since the idea of evolution gained a strong foothold in the Western world, and science and religion have mostly been at loggerheads with each other. Lately there has, however, been a renewed interest in this approach, which appears to be building further momentum.

I am referring to a new version of the Argument of Design. This 'argument' once was one of the most popular traditional proofs for the existence of God. Ever since the Middle Ages, philosophers and theologians have proposed a number of arguments which were regarded as 'proofs' for the idea that there is a God. They were mostly variants on one particular philosophical theme: every effect must have a cause, and every cause must be greater than its effect, and ultimately there must be a First Cause at the beginning of the causal chain. And, so the argument ran, if we can form an idea about a God who is eternal, almighty and all-knowing, this cannot originate without some cause. And we may refer to this cause as 'God', for such an idea cannot spring forth from our limited mind, because it must be caused by a Cause that exceeds its effect – the idea which we have formed. Furthermore, if we discern some general moral laws which are widely shared by humankind, this can only be explained by the fact that there is One who has initiated these moral principles.

The most famous version of this 'argument' ran like this: If we trek through the forest and suddenly discover a house with a well-kept garden, we shall assume that someone must have built the house and laid out the garden. Also, if we consider the intricate clockwork of a watch, we do not speculate that the watch might have come about through some kind of mysterious spontaneous generation, but we assume that a watchmaker of flesh and blood has been at work. This leads to the next step: If we study the universe and find that there is a definite order, we cannot reasonably avoid the conclusion that there must be a Maker who has put the cosmos and the world in that particular order. Or to put it in other words: Whenever there is evidence of *design* we must postulate a *designer*!

This argument for design was mothballed in most circles when the theory of evolution, in some form or another, gained almost universal acceptance. Charles Darwin (1809-1882) was not the first person to advance the hypothesis of a gradual evolvement of the various forms of life, from the simple to the very complex, through purely natural means. Before he wrote his famous *Origin of the Species,* others had already noticed that fossils of the simpler forms of life were buried in the oldest deposited layers of the earth, while fossilized remains of more advanced forms of life tended to be found in more recent sediments. But Darwin's name was to be forever linked to the evolutionary hypothesis, and others built on the foundation he laid with his notion of the 'survival of the fittest' during long periods in which the various forms of life adjusted to their environment.

Christians had a difficult time dealing with the 'scientific' explanation of the beginning and this gradual development of life. They were familiar with the biblical story of the creation of the world, including plants, and trees, fishes and birds, vertebrates and human beings – Adam and Eve – in six 24-hour periods, some 6,000, or at most 10,000, years ago. How were they to reconcile the new scientific data, and the words of men, however learned they might be, with the 'Word of God'? Some held tenaciously to a literal reading of the biblical narrative of a literal creation in six days. Others suggested that the early chapters of the Bible were mythical; they indicated, they said, that God had something to do with the origin of all things, but we must turn to the scientists for an explanation of the actual mechanics of the creation of the world and of life itself. Others again have proposed all kinds of compromise solutions, in feverish attempts to do justice both to the Bible and to science.

Evolutionary theory, with its alleged time span of hundreds of millions of years, still has a large part of the market when it comes to the ways in which people believe things came about. And those scholars are still regarded by many as pseudo-scientists when they argue that a 'recent creation' in a very short time by a divine Power is just as credible. However, change seems to in the air. In the last few decades quite a few scientists – astronomers, physicists and even biologists – have become more modest in their claims. They have come to the realization that some of the very foundational ideas of modern science are not quite as certain as a previous generation of scientists believed them to be. There are, for instance, small particles which do not behave in the way the laws of nature predicted. Scholars are also increasingly recognizing that science may not always be as objective as we have been told to believe. For scientists tend to look at the objects they study in a particular way, with particular instruments, and this may well, at least to a degree, influence the results of their enquiries. It is now widely accepted that many of our classical theories do not adequately support new findings, and that, as the tension builds between what we once considered a solid theoretical framework and all kinds of new ideas and discoveries, the 'old' framework may at some point have to be exchanged for a new scientific umbrella which will do a better job in holding our growing knowledge together.[4]

There is an increasing number of scientists who are willing to admit that the evolutionary hypothesis is just that: a hypothesis, which leaves a wide array of phenomena unexplained. In fact, it is argued by a number of authors that the evolution theory is in deep trouble.[5] There seems to be a greater readiness than before to accept that evolutionists operate with an unreasonable bias when they exclude *a priori* any non-natural explanation for the complex problems they cannot solve. And it begins to dawn on many who have been reading about the ongoing debate of faith versus evolution that, although many data can be explained by the theory of macroevolution, there are also many problems which defy an evolutionary explanation, while the idea of an intelligent creator may in actual fact do a better job at explaining many of the issues.[6]

Explaining the origin of life

Philosophically speaking, one might say that there are three possibilities in explaining the origin of the universe and, in particular, of life. Firstly, there is *chance*. This has been the classical Darwinian approach. If we allow for very long periods of time, chance will at some point in time bring the necessary building blocks of life together, and this first 'simple' form of life will then, over time, result in all the forms of life that have lived in the past and are living today on this planet. This approach has run into some serious difficulties. For we now know that there is no such thing as a 'simple' form of life, or even a 'simple' cell. Modern science has made it clear that cells and molecules possess a mind-boggling complexity, and the laws of statistics indicate that chance cannot be the ultimate explanation. As a result many feel that all chance-based theories must be rejected.

Secondly, there is the concept of *necessity* as an approach to the question of origins. This gives expression to the idea that everything that is, is the result of natural laws, a view that was quite popular for a while. When Napoleon asked astronomer Pierre Simon LaPlace (1749-1827) about the place he attributed to God in his theory of the origin of the heavenly bodies, LaPlace responded with the famous words: 'Sire, I have no need of this hypothesis.' He was convinced that physical laws had of necessity produced the universe and everything therein, and vehemently denied any suggestion that there might be anything beyond these laws.

Thirdly, there is the concept of *intelligent design* as a final explanation for the origin of the universe and of life on this planet. The well-known British physicist Paul Davies said in 1988 in his book *The Cosmic Blueprint*[7] what numerous scientists have also come to confess in various ways: 'The Impression of Design is overwhelming!' Let us briefly look at a few examples of the complexity in nature which have brought more and more scientists to the point that they can think of an explanation for the origin of the cosmos and of life only in terms of some form of intelligent design.

The fine tuning of the universe

In the last four or five decades, science has made it abundantly clear that the existence of life in the universe depends on a highly improbable but precise balance of physical factors. A wide range of circumstances must converge at the right time, in the right manner, in order to make the origin of life for humans possible. This is often referred to as the 'fine tuning' of the universe. It has been calculated that the chance for this to happen 'by accident' is somewhere in the region of ten billion multiplied by itself 123 times.[8] It is, therefore, given this staggering improbability, difficult *not* to assume that some form of intelligence was involved in the creation of life! We find this confirmed when we look at the infinite complexity of the building blocks for human life, the cell and DNA.

Speaking of a 'simple' cell is no longer possible. A cell can be compared to a factory with an elaborate network of assembly lines. Maybe Carl Sagan (1934-1996) overstated his case when he said that a 'simple' cell contains an amount of information comparable to about a hundred million pages of printed material. Let's assume that Richard Dawkins, the well-known British biologist, who continues to ridicule the belief in any kind of creation, is nearer to the truth when he claims that a cell 'only' has information equal to thirty volumes of the *Encyclopaedia Britannica*. Even if Dawkins is right, there is clearly nothing 'primitive' about the 'simple' cell.[9]

DNA is somewhat like computer software, but it is much more complicated than anything we can find in the marketplace of human-made IT-products. It is a storage system for information that far exceeds anything human intelligence has been able to produce. If you know but little about the intricacies of the DNA and think that is a strong statement, I dare you to go to your local library and consult a recent encyclopaedia, or to surf the Internet for a while. I am sure you will return to this chapter with a sense of astonishment or even bewilderment. If DNA carries such an abundance of information, it is far harder, it seems to me, to believe that this is the result of mere chance than to assume that somehow a superior intelligence plays the decisive role.

But this is only a small part of the story of complexity. Apart from the fascinating and complex structures found within the cells of our bodies, we find that these cells constitute quite distinct classes of tissue: cardiac, smooth muscle, striated muscle, epidermal, etc. At a higher level we may study the extremely complex organs: heart, lungs, liver, gall bladder, spleen, skin and brain, etc, and the various systems: circulatory, respiratory, urinary, nervous, skeletal, muscular. These organs and systems work together in totally integrated processes. And, of course, it does not stop there. The individual animals and human beings form a complex interrelated community. And beyond these, the earth and its living organisms exist together in a great network of complex interactions. The oxygen used by animals is produced by the photosynthesis in the plant world, and the animals release carbon dioxide which the plants need. And to cap it all, the earth exists in a complex arrangement of planets, asteroids, moons, suns and other stars and galaxies, in such a way as to allow life on earth to exist and persist.[10] It surely all points to some kind of intelligent design.

The eye

Several authors who in recent years have written about the difficulties in the evolutionary theory have focused on the eye. They have stressed the improbability that such a delicate organ developed over millions of years, from a 'simple' light sensitive spot to the intricate human eye. (And note that this leaves the vexing question unanswered: of what use would an eye be to any creature as long as it was still in the process of producing vision? How would an eye-in-process without any vision be of any real use in the struggle for survival during this long period of hundreds of thousands or millions of years of evolutionary adaptation?)

Even Darwin himself realized that his theory could not in a credible way account for the evolution of the eye. The biologists in the late nineteenth century already knew that the eye was a complex structure, with many components, such as a lens, a retina, tear ducts, oscular muscles, etc. But they had no idea what would be needed to produce a light-sensitive spot. Nor did they have the foggiest idea of what happens when a photon of light impinges upon a retina. I have tried to understand what is involved, but must admit that it is all far beyond my grasp of anatomy, biology and chemistry. Please try to read the following quotation in full and do not stop after the first few difficult terms:

'When a photon first hits the retina, it interacts with a small organic molecule called 11-cis-retinal. The shape of retinal is rather bent, but when retinal interacts with the photon, it straightens out, isomerizing into trans-retinal. This is the signal that sets in motion a whole cascade of events resulting in vision. When retinal changes shape, it forces a change in the shape of the rhodopsin, which is bound to it. The change in the rhodopsin's shape exposes a binding site that allows the protein transducin to stick to it. Now part of the transducin dissociates and interacts with a protein called phosphodiesterase. When that happens, the phosphodiesterase acquires the ability chemically to cut a small organic molecule called cyclic-GMP, turning it into 5'-GMP. There is a lot of cyclic-GMP in the cell, and some of it sticks to another protein called an ion channel. Normally the ion channel allows sodium ions into the cell. When the concentration of the cyclic-GMP decreases because of the action of the phosphodiesterase, however, the cyclic-GMP bound to the ion channel eventually falls off, causing a change in shape that shuts the channel. As a result, sodium ions can no longer enter the cell, the concentration of sodium in the cell decreases, and the voltage across the cell membrane changes. This in turn causes a wave of electrical polarization to be sent down the optic nerve to the brain. And, when interpreted by the brain, that is vision.'[11]

I realize that for most readers (as for me) this is far too specialized to appreciate. But to me this does not sound like the language of *chance*. This rather sounds like referring to something that was planned and was carefully constructed. It has *design* written all over it.

Enough proof?

It is not difficult to find other examples of complexity in the world of nature which point to intelligent design. It is therefore rather strange that so many still refuse to entertain the possibility that there is some form of intelligent design. True, no CNN-reporter was there to make sure that the entire world would instantaneously know about it. But we were not there either when the faces of the four American presidents were cut out in the rocks of Mount Rushmore in South Dakota. Yet I do not know of any scientist who would deny that these rocky portraits were the result of intelligent design. Even if we had not known that sculptor Gutzon Borglum began drilling into the 5,725-foot mountain in 1927 and spent fourteen years in creating his work of art, we would have concluded that someone had been there to create this magnificent monument to democracy.

No one alive today believes that the hieroglyphs on the famous Rosetta Stone, a compact basalt slab which was discovered in July 1799 and is now one of the important attractions of the British Museum in London, came about by some freak accident. Someone in antiquity with a mind was the creator.

The astounding element we discover in nature may actually not so much be the *order*, but rather the enormous *complexity* that points to intelligent design. Yet, while most people are willing to acknowledge intelligent design when they see an artefact or document with far less complexity than they find in the cell and in DNA, many are strangely unwilling to accept intelligent design when they look at the sheer infinite complexity of our universe, from the smallest particles which are as yet invisible to the naked eye, to the zillion luminous and other bodies in the universe of which we are but an infinitesimal part.

True enough, we may never have absolute proof. But how absolute does our 'proof' have to be? In normal life we are satisfied with common-sense conclusions. When we detect fingerprints, we assume someone has been there and has touched the place where his prints are left. Why then is it so difficult for so many to accept that a Superior Intelligence – God – has clearly left his fingerprints on the world around us?

The words of Ariel Roth, a Christian biologist and geologist, are worth quoting:

'The data related to the origin of life favour the idea of a mastermind and a directed non-random process involved in the creation of life on earth. If we choose to eliminate the concept of a Creator, we have little choice but to accept some kind of chemical evolution, but the scientific data against such concepts are so compelling that reason would suggest that we explore other alternatives.'[12]

Is there a God who gives meaning to our existence? We have briefly looked at that question from the inside out and from the outside in. I have focused your attention on that mysterious feeling of ultimate dependence which was, and is, so extremely widespread, in the past and present, around the world. It will not go away. It forces itself upon most of us with a mysterious certainty. How can it just be a fruit of wishful thinking or mere imagination? That certainly is not the first common-sense conclusion that forces itself upon us. We have also taken a brief but intensive look at the complexity of the universe and of human life, and have considered the clear indications of intelligent design.

Which of those two approaches provides the stronger argument for the existence of a Someone who is beyond us all and has left his imprint on our world and on life as we know it? It may be that the outside-in approach, which so strongly points to intelligent design, is the more convincing. But the inside-out approach does, I believe, give additional support to the idea that there is a God. For if there is an intelligent design and a Designer, it stands to reason that he would at least leave some trace of his existence in his ultimate design of human beings.

If, on the basis of all of this, we do not deny outright that there is a God but are at least open to the possibility that there is, we will have made an important first step in our journey of discovery. Because this means that life may not be meaningless. There seems to be an intricate design, which presupposes a Designer. There could be purpose to life. To my life. If there is a God, we are not here by accident. We are meant to be here. Camus was wrong: Life is more than a game.

But to say that there is good reason to believe that there must be a Designer-God is one thing. To define this God further is quite another thing. Can we *know* anything about him with any certainty? If he exists, can we find out what he is like, what he does and what he does not do? What he wants and what he does not want? The next chapter will address these questions, as we move from the issue of meaning to that of Truth. As we do so, I recognize that even the word truth – let alone when used with a capital T – is a highly uncomfortable term for most post-modern people. But let's give it a try.

Chapter two

Truth

When the United States of America declared its independence on 4 July 1776, its future was still highly uncertain. But about some things the founding fathers were sure. They believed there were a number of foundational truths on which the new nation would be built. These 'truths' were held to be 'self-evident', as their famous Declaration of Independence indicated. They were *absolute truths* which needed no further argumentation or defence.

Indeed, until quite recently, most people had no problem with the concept of absolute, or self-evident, truths. But in recent times this has changed dramatically. Absolute certainty about a series of basic beliefs and convictions rings hollow with many of us today. As Alan Bloom wrote in his bestselling analysis of the changes in American thinking: 'There is one thing a professor can be absolutely certain of: almost every student entering the university believes, or says he believes, that truth is relative'.[13]

One of the main characteristics of postmodernism is the view that Truth no longer exists. Truth has become a matter of personal belief, of social custom. Truth is not something universally valid, something that counts whatever the circumstances, but has developed into what I, as an individual, or what we, as a particular group, happen to believe. Notice the tremendous shift that has taken place: In the past (that is, even just a few decades ago!) people argued about the differences between belief systems. They pointed to the multitude of Christian churches and wanted to know which of them was right. But that question is something of the past.

The issue is now rather whether there is, in fact, any Truth at all. For many this is a question that has been answered with a resounding 'no'. They will say that absolute Truth is a fiction. It has been replaced with less authoritative notions. Instead of building on a sure foundation of Truth, we have points of view, opinions and impressions.[14]

To theologians, church leaders and church members of the more conservative variety, all of this sounds like total heresy. For what will remain of faith, and of the church, if there is no Truth? Douglas Groothuis, a professor at a conservative Christian seminary in the USA, is one of those who are horribly alarmed by this development. He speaks of the 'decay' of Truth.[15] He and others warn that the demise of Truth does not only bring havoc to Christian creeds and doctrines, which supposedly provide authoritative expressions of the Truth of the Bible, but also to morality. For if there is no Absolute Truth, they keep emphasizing, there is no absolute distinction between right and wrong, good and evil. It all becomes a matter of consensus, of preference. It becomes a matter of what benefits me or the group to which I belong. This has profound implications for such concepts as justice and human rights. Groothuis asserts that without some kind of foundational Truth any kind of thinking and behaving, however bizarre, becomes legitimate.[16]

How did Truth become truths?

Considering the dramatic changes in our world in the last half century or so, it is hardly surprising that the way in which more and more people look at the world has also changed. Until a generation or so ago only a happy few (and from only a handful of countries) were able to travel abroad and to meet with people from different cultures. In most areas of the world the reigning culture was the standard by which people lived. If they knew about other cultures, it was seldom from actual experience. The postmodern person in the Western world, however, not only travels to faraway places on other continents with less hassle than it took his forbears to make a train journey across the continental United States or across Western Europe, but he also lives in a multicultural society. She no longer inhabits a monocultural Christian world, but is part of a highly pluralistic society with people of all colours of skin, and with a vast variety of cultures and languages. It is a world in which Islam and other world religions thrive, while most Christian denominations have lost a major percentage of their active membership, especially in Western Europe. In addition, we are today bombarded with so much information from an almost infinite array of sources, in particular via the Internet, that it has become extremely challenging to know what is truth or fiction, let alone what can be considered the *absolute truth*.

The postmodern person, it is claimed, has difficulty knowing who he is, because he lives such a fragmented life. When someone would ask Jacques Derrida (1930-2004), one of the foremost philosophers of postmodernism: 'How are you?', he would answer: 'On what floor?' He compared our human existence with 'living in a house, but on different floors.' Our life consists of layers, or compartments, which hardly interconnect. Our personal world is subdivided into a number of separate spheres – home, work, recreation (and sometimes church); – and the ways in which people act, and even the ethical norms they operate with, depend on the compartment they happen to be in (the 'floor' where they happen to be) at a particular moment.

These developments lend quite a bit of plausibility to the postmodern philosophies for many people in today's Western world and lead them to embrace the concept of relativity. But the roots of this shift from absolute truth to personal truths reach a lot further than just the last few decades. The German philosopher Friedrich Nietzsche (1844-1900) played a key role in this process. This son of a Lutheran pastor is probably best known for his radical rejection of the Christian faith and the Christian church. He was the first writer to refer enthusiastically to the 'death of God'. But this was just one aspect of his 'deconstructive' thinking. He became the father of later postmodern philosophers in stating that there are no real facts but only interpretations of facts! We can never touch the real thing, he said, but must always be content with our own private interpretation of it.

The idea that we can never get hold of absolute truth or pure reality was also one of the main contentions of the philosophy of language of the late nineteenth and much of the twentieth century. It was argued by several prominent philosophers of language that language does not help us in our search for absolute truth, since the meaning of language depends to a large extent on the group to which one happens to belong. Every social group agrees with how words are used and what meaning they have. The famous Ludwig Wittgenstein (1889-1951) said that each social group plays its own 'language game'. Postmodern philosophers have picked up on this, and have applied this in particular to the written texts of the past. They ask: How do we know what the original authors intended to say? How was what they said coloured by their worldview? How do we, who read these texts today, find meaning for our own life in what these authors said? How do we, in our own context and with our own biases, read their words and find meaning? They conclude that a text has as many meanings as it has readers; each reader determines for himself what a text means and one interpretation has as much validity as any other.

One of the foremost postmodern thinkers, Jean François Lyotard (1924-1998), added another ingredient to this cocktail of uncertainty and relativism. In 1979 he received a request from the authorities in Quebec to produce a survey of the state of knowledge in the most highly developed societies. The publication of his book *The Postmodern Condition: A Report on Knowledge* placed postmodernism on the intellectual map. In this book and in several of his other writings (which are quite dense and hard to read for the average human being), he points to the end of the 'grand stories.' This term stands for the *metanarratives*, the overarching systems of thought, which try to provide an all-encompassing explanation of our world and of what matters in society. These 'grand' stories, he says, are no longer credible. They only mask the obsession with power of those who promote these stories. Lyotard was thinking in particular of the 'grand story' of Marxism. He had personally witnessed the failure of Marxism in the North African context where he grew up and lived until the age of twenty-eight. He believed that the time for any such metanarratives had passed, whether it was Marxism, Communism, Capitalism or Christianity. All these metanarratives had been proclaimed as truth, but history had shown, Lyotard tells us, that they were no more than the cloak of power-hungry systems promoted by individuals or elitist groups, which would not eschew violence in order to reach their goals. We would do much better, Lyotard says, to live with 'smaller stories', which are far less ambitious, and even to accept the fact that these 'smaller stories' at times contradict one another. Once again we notice how the ideal of universal Truth was replaced by a multiplicity of truths!

Another prominent postmodern thinker, the American Richard Rorty (b. 1931), is just as sceptical regarding the possibility of arriving at anything resembling absolute truth. He no longer considers truth as something that designates reality, but takes an utterly pragmatic view. Truth, he says, is what gets things done. It has been pointed out by many critics that this remains a rather unsatisfactory approach, since it seems to accept all kinds of manipulative use of language which certainly 'got things done', including the horrendous acts committed by Nazis and Stalinists! But the moral of the story is the same: Absolute truth has been demoted to opportunistic truths.

Can we still hope to find Truth?

Many people in today's Western world, whether they have read these complicated philosophical books or not, tend to agree that these postmodern philosophers may possibly have a point in their rejection of absolute truth. They will point out that we can hardly deny that much has been paraded before us as truth, that later turned out to be no more than wishful thinking, propaganda or even deceit, and it is small wonder therefore that many instantly become sceptical whenever a new truth-candidate gets on the podium.

I shall never forget the first trips I made in the mid-1990s to Albania, the small country on the Balkan peninsula which had been totally isolated from the rest of the world until in 1992 the communist regime was finally forced to accept the new political reality of the post-communist era. Two things impressed me most: the total absence of any church buildings or mosques, and the ubiquitous small concrete shelters with a diameter of some 8-10 metres that stood 4 to 5 feet above the ground. I learned that there were enough of these saucer-like shelters to enable all Albanians (about 3.5 million of them) to seek cover when the enemy came to raid Albania in search of its riches. For, so dictator Enver Hoxha (1908-1985) had told his people, Albania was the richest nation on earth, and it would be only a matter of time until some enemy would come and try to take away the immense Albanian wealth. This was the truth for the Albanian people. But as soon as some of them, somehow, were able to get their hands on satellite equipment and to receive Italian television programmes, and when, a little later, the borders opened, and they were beginning to travel, they were completely disillusioned. They had been totally manipulated by the political propaganda of a small elite which desperately clung to power for as long as it could. The 'Truth' proved to be a malicious lie.

Even in the domain of science, the search for truth is not always as 'clean' and straightforward as we are often asked to believe. Research may be sponsored by particular industries which hope that the outcome of the research will be to their benefit. Findings which do not fit into the desired scenario may not always be reported as fully as they should. Grants do not necessarily go to the best scientists and to the research programmes that are in greatest need of additional finance. Networking and political skills play a considerable role in getting financial backing. Furthermore, no scientist is a *tabula rasa* as he starts out on his search for truth. He comes to his field of study with assumptions and biases, and is easily predisposed to look in a particular direction.

All of this also applies in the field of religion, the domain *par excellence* of truth – of the things of ultimate concern. Theologians are supposed to study and communicate the truth. Churches are to protect and to preach the truth. But rather than a unified message of truth, we hear a cacophony of theological opinions and, instead of one firm ecclesiastical voice, we are confronted with the confusing and contradictory truth claims of a myriad denominations and other religious organizations. The Bible can, it seems, be interpreted in so many different ways that it is able simultaneously to 'prove' positions that are diametrically opposed. And, regrettably, we also often discover a dark side to the Christian truth: manipulation, power-play, cover-ups and sloppy thinking.

Does this reality not suggest that it makes sense for us to join in this postmodern rejection of absolute truth? For even in places where we expect to have the best chances of finding it (science, religion), we not only face philosophical objections but also some real practical hurdles. Why spend time and effort in chasing a phantom?

But let's not give up too soon! For what would be the implication if there were no absolute truth but only truths (opinions, preferences, opinions)? The alternative of total relativism is not very appealing. And, indeed, it may be difficult to arrive at absolute truth, but common sense demands, nonetheless, that we acknowledge certain principles of logic. For starters, I believe we must acknowledge that two or more statements which flatly contradict each other cannot be simultaneously true. In other words: Not all propositions can be true. Some are true and some are not.

Admittedly, some things will remain a matter of preference or opinion. I happen to be interested in contemporary art. Even though many pieces of twentieth and twenty-first century art (this is especially true of much postmodern art) at first sight appear weird, they may nevertheless be very interesting. And there are pieces which I consider not only interesting but beautiful. Others may completely disagree with me and will wonder how such meaningless 'junk' could end up in a museum gallery. They may even be angry that tax-payers probably provided at least some of the money for acquiring a particular piece of art. Who is right? Obviously, appreciation of artistic expressions remains a matter of individual preference, and propositions about the beauty of a painting, a sculpture or some other object of art do not answer to the category of right or wrong.

But if I say that Amsterdam is the capital of the Netherlands, and my neighbour argues for Brussels as the capital of the Netherlands, it is a different matter. In this case I am absolutely right and my neighbour is totally wrong. It is not just a matter of perspective, opinion or interpretation of an atlas, but a matter of fact, as every Dutch and Belgian citizen will be able to tell you.

Let us take this a step further. When I say that the horse that I see across the road from where I live is black and my neighbour says that the horse is dark brown, it may not immediately be clear who is right. The horse may *seem* black to me, whereas it is actually dark brown. I may be a little colour blind or may simply not have put my glasses on. We may have to go outside and get closer to the horse in order to determine the exact shade of his colour. In this case we may be able to check physically which statement was true. But there are many instances where we cannot actually check the truth of a proposition until we receive some additional evidence (from an actual witness) that helps us settle the matter. But we shall agree that one of the propositions may be right, or that all propositions in question may be wrong and that, if they make mutually exclusive claims, not all of them can be right. In some instances it may just be a matter of being able to travel somewhere or of having the right instruments, or enough time, to bring the matter to a satisfactory solution. In many other cases we shall have to defer judgement.

Of course, things become more complicated when we are dealing with statements which do not allow for any physical checking. Christians make certain truth claims for their viewpoints, and Muslims or adherents to other religions also present certain truth claims about their faith. Some of these truth claims are identical or very similar. They may, therefore, be true or not. We do not have the possibility to check the truth content of most of these claims. For instance, both Christianity and Islam tell us that there is an afterlife of eternal bliss. But, obviously, none of us has ever been there and can testify that there is indeed such a happy life hereafter, and none of us has ever spoken to anyone (who appears to be sane), who has actually been there and has come back with a series of digital pictures. However, there are also truth claims in which Christians differ greatly from Muslims. In such instances Christians and Muslims may both be wrong. But they cannot both be right. When Christians, for instance, state that the *Bible* is the book that contains what God wants to communicate to us, and when Muslims say that it is the *Koran* that contains the ultimate divine instruction, we cannot have it both ways, and one of the statements must be false.

This again takes us one step further. If we are willing to 'buy' the idea that total relativism seems unjustified since common-sense logic teaches us that propositions may actually be true or false, and that in certain cases we may, in fact, be able to determine whether statements can be accepted as true or false, we may want to ask whether we can somehow, somewhere, find a basis of indubitable truth on which we can build further and which may give us clues as to the possible truth of other propositions. If that is indeed our next thought we can hardly claim any originality, for this has been a quest of many centuries. The technical term for this desire to establish a firm foundation of basic truth is referred to as *Foundationalism*. If we can be sure that our words refer to a Reality that we can somehow, at least in part, know, we have made a promising start in our pursuit of further knowledge. If we can somehow establish, beyond reasonable doubt, that there is a God and that he is the Designer of the universe and the Creator of life, it would appear that we have a foundation on which we can build. And if we can, at the same time, beyond reasonable doubt, be sure that there is an ancient text which contains truth from this God, then, I believe, we shall be able to make considerable progress in our quest for further information about this God.

Is it possible to get that kind of certainty? Most present-day thinkers do not believe that Foundationalism is defensible. In fact, there are many voices which suggest that the metaphor of a 'foundation' of absolute truth is not the most suitable word picture. Karl Popper (1902-1994), W. V. O. Quine (1908-2000) and others have suggested that it might be better to use the image of a 'net' or 'web' as we try to picture how we acquire and systematize knowledge. Rather than starting with a few absolute building blocks which serve as the foundation for our further thinking, we would do better, they say, to look for all kinds of different strands of argument and evidence, that come to us from many different directions – as in a web – but form a coherent story in which separate beliefs are strengthened by their ties to other beliefs and to the whole. Even though the various strands of evidence may not be fully convincing when considered in isolation from one another, together they may enable us to arrive, if not at absolute truth, then at 'justifiable belief'. And that may be the most we can hope to achieve.[17]

Truth about God

Personally, I agree, after a lot of reading and thinking, with the conclusion that the image of a 'web' appears indeed to be more convincing than that of a 'foundation'. Usually, the foundations that have been identified are only fully convincing to those who are already disposed to consider them as foundational. But this does not mean that there is no *truth*. I strongly suggest that the issues we discussed in the previous chapter – the evidences of intelligent design which so clearly point to an Intelligent Designer, and the remarkable phenomenon of a profound sense of absolute dependence which is found among people of all ages and in so many cultures – are powerful threads in this web of knowledge. Moreover, as we shall see in subsequent chapters, there are many other threads that can be woven into this web – into a coherent system of justifiable belief.

As we look for further truth about this intelligent Designer and this 'Mysterious Ground of our Being' on whom so many say they depend in some ultimate way, we have to make sure that we avoid a fundamental misunderstanding. There is an immense difference between *believing in absolutes* and *having some absolute belief* about everything. There are many puzzles we may never solve and there are many things we do not need to be absolutely certain about. But there is one basic consideration: If there is a God who stands at the beginning of everything, this God is obviously infinitely more powerful and more knowledgeable than any human being or even collective humanity. If there is such a God, we must expect there to be a great gap, possibly unbridgeable, between him and us. And we shall in all likelihood always be left with questions. Many things may simply remain beyond us, and in many cases we shall be left with conjectures. There may be less truth that we can understand than we expected or hoped for. And we would do well to be extremely sceptical towards those who claim they have the complete truth about God. Many of them are totally closed to any dialogue that questions the slightest aspect of their truth. They 'see themselves as God's self-appointed police force, guardians of truth who perceive themselves as wearing a "badge of divinity" upon their own theological system.'[18] Furthermore, we must always remember, as we probe this matter of truth, that we never come to the table without our own personal histories, our own knowledge and experiences. We see things through the educational and cultural lenses we have acquired. We can never totally shake off our preconceived opinions. We do not have what is often termed a 'God's-eye' perspective that sees in complete objectivity everything in its pure relationship to everything else.

But I am convinced that this does not condemn us to utter relativism. For, as we saw earlier in this chapter, the laws of logic tell us that not all propositions can be correct, and this implies that not all propositions about religion and about God can be correct either. To take an obvious example: There are many different, and conflicting, opinions about Jesus Christ, the Centre of Christianity; not all of them can be true at the same time. The classical Christian position from the dawn of the church's history onward, which is still believed by 'orthodox' Christians today, has been that Jesus was not just a human person, but was of divine origin. He was God in human form. Whatever all of this may mean exactly, it is clear that if this classical Christian claim is true, he was not just a prophet (as the Muslims believe), or a misguided reformer (as the Jews believe), or an *atavar* of Brahman (as the Hindus believe), or a God-realized guru (as the New Age enthusiasts believe); or an inspired but not divine social prophet (as many 'liberal' Christians believe), etc.[19]

Or to take another classical Christian conviction: God is a Personal Being and consists of an indivisible unity of Father, Son and Holy Spirit. Let us at this point not worry about the extremely difficult concept of the Trinity – 'threeness in oneness' and 'oneness in threeness' – which cannot adequately be put into human language. But if this is true, the basic concepts about God that are held by Muslims, Jews, Hindus, Buddhists, New Age adherents, animists and polytheists cannot also be true, for many of the ideas held in these non-Christian religions flatly contradict what Christians say about God. Even if Christianity does not have it right, only one (or none) of the others will be correct.

So, not everything that may be suggested about God or any other religious topic is, I think, a matter of personal preference or truth. It may be difficult or impossible to know the answers to all kinds of questions about God; I feel we must insist that not all answers are equally valid, for the simple reason that they are often mutually exclusive in what they propose. What, then, is the way forward in our quest for truth? How can we weave another thread in our 'web' that fits coherently with the threads that are already there?

Divine communication?

If there is a God who is at the beginning of everything, including human life, it would be strange if this God does not somehow want to communicate some truth about himself to the creatures he designed – the more so, since language and interpersonal communication is such a dominant feature in the design of these human creatures. The idea that this Designer-God would somehow reveal himself to the creatures that owe their existence to him is quite believable, once you accept that God's existence falls into the category of 'justifiable beliefs'. But how would this divine-human communication take place? One prerequisite would be that he would have to make use of the kind of language and symbols that these humans would understand. That would, of course, place a serious restriction on the content of the communication, considering the inevitable inequality between Sender and receiver. Yet it would also imply that human talk about God can have real meaning; after all, God's deployment of human words and symbols in reference to himself means that these words are not mere human constructs but do represent an objective reality outside of man's own world. (It is important to make this point, since many of the postmodern philosophers have expressed major doubt as to whether what we say only concerns the things as we experience them, or can also refer to a reality which is beyond our immediate reach.)

How would these divine communications reach us? Would they come as impressions to feed our intuition and our conscience? Would they come via dreams or extrasensory perceptions? Would God actually use audible speech? Or would he prefer somehow to put his communications in writing and make them available through some authoritative text that we could read and contemplate? All or at least several of these channels of communication are recognized as possibilities by different major world religions, even though there are momentous differences among them regarding the content of what has allegedly been communicated. Several of the world religions (most notably Judaism, Islam and Christianity) base their teachings on a sacred text which they believe was initiated (inspired) by God but actually written by human hands. There are different theories as to how that was supposed to have happened and how much influence those human instruments actually exerted on the content of the communication.

So, can a sacred text like the Bible or the Koran possibly help us in our search for truth? Is there any reason to believe that a book can reveal important facts about this Designer God – about who he is and what he is, what he does and how he relates to what he designed? If he 'spoke' to people who then wrote down what he said, how can we be sure that what he 'said' was faithfully transmitted, and that it still has relevancy for us who live thousands of years after these texts were written by God's 'penmen'? And what book should we choose? Even if we narrow the choice down to the most widespread of these texts, the Koran and the Bible, why choose the Bible? This is an important question, for in the rest of the book I intend to refer to the Bible numerous times.

An extraordinary book

There are a few basic reasons why I regard the Bible as a very special book from which I believe I can learn about God and which informs me about how he affects my life. I want to list them briefly. I realize that many of you who read this will not be able to judge whether these arguments hold much water until you yourselves do a considerable amount of reading *about* the Bible and *in* the Bible. But even then it will be necessary to proceed on a preliminary basis. For to agree that the Bible is a most extraordinary book is one thing, but to claim that it contains trustworthy (absolutely true) information about God (truth) goes quite a bit further. Let us, however, look at a few remarkable facts that make the Bible stand out from all other books, even from other so-called 'holy' books like the Koran.

First of all, the Bible has an extraordinary track record. It is easily the most printed, most translated, most read, and probably most discussed book in human history. Its full text is now available in well over 2,000 languages, with parts of it in many more languages or dialects. In comparison, William Shakespeare, considered by many to be the master writer of the English language, has been translated into only fifty languages. No one really knows how many copies of the Bible have been printed since the invention of movable print in the fifteenth century. A reasonably careful estimate is around 7 billion copies! So I am certainly not alone, or part of a small minority, in my high regard for the Bible. Of course, the fact that a given book has had more readers than any other book in itself proves very little about its truth. But it does raise our curiosity about the book.

Secondly, the remarkable thing about this book is not only that it is a multi-authored book, although that is certainly noteworthy. The sixty-six different segments of the Bible were written by some forty different authors from all walks of life: shepherds, farmers, tent-makers, physicians, fishermen, priests, philosophers and kings. These authors were for the most part not contemporaries, but many of them lived centuries apart. The earliest parts of their writings date from the fifteenth century BC, while the final contribution was written around AD100. From the fourth century onwards there was general consensus that these sixty-six tracts belonged in the Bible. But – and that is nothing less than miraculous – despite those differences in education, occupation and social status of the authors and the span of years it took to write it (in three different languages: Hebrew, Aramaic or Greek), and to establish it as one collection, the Bible is an extremely cohesive and unified book. Its sixty-six segments constitute a book with one unified philosophy. No wonder this has led hundreds of millions of people to conclude that the Bible must somehow be more than just a human creation.

Thirdly, the Bible proves to be remarkably accurate in its historical details. This comes as a surprise to many people. When, particularly in the nineteenth century, new theories about the origin of the Bible were gaining ground among theologians and also among church members, there was great doubt in the minds of many about the historical veracity of a lot of the details of the Bible story. Admittedly, there are still some statements which are difficult to fit into the history of the ancient world as we know it today, and which continue to puzzle historians. But by and large the accuracy of the historical statements of the Bible has been vindicated. Biblical archeology has time and again demonstrated that the men and women mentioned in the Bible were, indeed, historical figures, and that the deeds attributed to them in the Bible did, indeed, take place in the way they are described.

Fourthly, there is the astonishing phenomenon of prophecy. In everyday parlance, 'prophecy' has to do with predictions. In the Bible the term prophecy has a much broader meaning, but the Bible prophets also made many statements about the future, often about events that were still hundreds of years away. There are, for instance, many dozens, if not hundreds, of statements in the writings of the first major 'compartment' of the Bible (the Old Testament) which provide details about the birth, the life and death of Jesus Christ, every one of which proved to be fully accurate.

As I said above, you should not take my word for all this, but you should do your own reading and thinking. But reading *about* the Bible should never take the place of reading the Bible itself.

This is, in fact, one of the major problems we face when we want to talk about the Bible. Even in the so-called Christian world, most people today are biblically illiterate. It becomes rather difficult to arrive at a balanced judgement about a book without having read it. (That, of course, is just as true when we pronounce final judgement on other 'sacred' books, like the Koran).

But there is more. Some well-known Bible experts have stated that the arguments I have listed above are not the most important ones. They say that the crux of the matter is that the Bible speaks for itself when you start reading it, or, to use a technical term, it is *self-authenticating*. That means, in more common language, that there is something in the Bible that convinces us deep down that it has a unique dimension which demands our attention, and that it contains more than human words.

Indeed, it stands to reason that if God should bother to provide us with information of some sort, he would call our attention to the source that he has provided. I would definitely agree with that. This certainly strengthens the points I mentioned about the Bible in the previous paragraphs as important additional 'threads' in our 'web' of basic knowledge.

Reading the Bible will often be rather challenging. If you open a Bible for the first time and decide to read it from cover to cover, you may get stuck in passages which are, to put it mildly, not easily accessible. It may therefore be advisable to start with some of the easier sections, for instance with one of the four short biographies of Jesus,[20] and then move on to other historical sections. It is also advisable to read an introduction to the Bible, which provides some background information and explains that not all of the Bible was written in one and the same style. Some sections are historical prose; others are poetry or deploy yet another literary style. It is important to be aware of such basic facts.

Bible reading remains challenging even for the advanced reader. For, even if one *believes* (see next chapter) that God communicates with humans through the pages of the Bible, it is nonetheless quite clear that in many ways the text of the Bible shares in the characteristics of other ancient texts. The authors expressed what they were 'inspired' to say with the words and symbols they were familiar with, within the context of their own world-view. When we read these words today, we must not only try to discover the essential meaning of what was expressed in words and symbols which may no longer be ours, but must also be conscious of the fact that we approach these ancient words with our own twenty-first century presuppositions, against the background of our modern or postmodern thinking. We tend to read our own presuppositions and culture back into the text. The postmodern philosopher who tells us that there are as many meanings to a text as there are readers certainly has a point. Yet I strongly believe that if you put time and effort into it, and are also willing to listen to what others around you have discovered as they do their best to apply the old words to their present situation, you will notice that these old words still possess a remarkable power to speak to us today.

I do not know of one single person who claims to understand every biblical passage. There is always more to learn and there are always greater depths to probe. It is, however, the experience of many that the Bible continues to speak to the reader, and constantly 'reveals' further depth and meaning, even after he has read a particular section for the umpteenth time. Many readers in days past and also today will underline that, even if they cannot understand everything or find some statement hard to swallow, the Bible offers a more cogent view of the world, of life, of human existence than any other book they have read. They have found that it offers a cohesive and satisfying alternative for postmodern relativity. They have concluded that it points to a universe that owes its origin to a Designer-God, who is also the ultimate objective Law-giver. As a result, they say, it can supply an absolute difference between right and wrong.

I agree. True enough, the Bible does not answer all our questions about life, suffering and death, but it does present the most coherent and convincing explanation for the human predicament. It also establishes the identity of Jesus Christ in the most articulate and satisfactory way. And it contains a recipe for a meaningful and satisfying life here and hereafter.

The biblical view best accounts for a whole range of facts (universe, humans, history) in accordance with the essential tenets of logic and criteria for evidence that are required for all critical thinking.[21] This is what millions of people have discovered as they read the Bible. Again, this is not hard scientific evidence that indubitably proves the Bible has a supernatural dimension, but is does lend further support to the 'justifiable belief' that the Designer-God has found an effective way of communicating with humans.

Believing truth

Many Christians who speak of 'truth' do not think only of the Bible, but also of a number of formal statements and documents which allegedly define aspects of this 'truth'. I am referring to the creeds of the various Christian churches and the traditional Christian doctrines. What is their status? Do they have the same standing as the Bible itself? For some Christians they do. Some, mostly subconsciously, may well be inclined to read the Bible in the light of such statements, rather than vice-versa. But I will propose in the next chapter that these documents and statements have a different function. The Bible is the source from which we collect the rough material for our doctrinal statements. They then systematize and summarize what we *believe* the Biblical view is with regard to important issues.

I hope many of you will leave this chapter with a sense that there is a lot to be said for the idea that there is more to consider than just preferences and opinions, and for the idea that a Designer-God has provided us with truth. We may lack a foundation which leaves no room for any doubt, but there clearly appears to be this 'web' in which the various threads reinforce one another, and the result may at least be called 'justifiable belief'. What is involved in this 'believing' is the theme for the next step in our discovery: *Faith*. Here the word 'leap' may well be more accurate than the word 'step'. Are you ready for it?

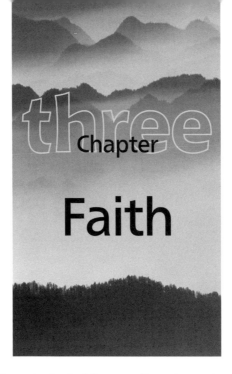

Chapter three

Faith

So far we have looked at the question of meaning and at the possibility of truth, and I hope this has brought as least some of you to come to some tentative conclusions. There is meaning to life if the world and all therein is the creative product of a Designer-God, a Supreme Source of our being on whom so many people feel ultimately dependent. But, as we said, it is one thing to accept this idea and even to accept the possibility or likelihood that this God – or whatever term we use for this 'Ground of our being' – decided to communicate with us, and then to proceed on the presupposition that the Bible is a key component in this communication – it is quite another thing to believe everything Christians in all their denominational varieties affirm about their God.

Christians differ in countless ways in their religious convictions. The existence of hundreds (or, if you include also many smaller ones, several thousands) of different denominations and of the various modalities within most denominations is a powerful reminder of that sad reality. But many, right across these denominational walls, would at least agree to a few basic convictions about some 'attributes' of God, about Jesus Christ and what he means for mankind, and about a mysterious entity which is referred to as the Holy Spirit. Yet to hold even those basic convictions is quite a step beyond what we discussed in the first two chapters. We might say, once again: it is a *leap*. It is indeed a gargantuan leap, but it is not a blind leap into the dark. Let's try to figure out in the following pages whether we have enough justification to take this leap.

How normal is faith?

Before we are ready to prepare ourselves for this leap, we must look at a preliminary question: Is it normal or abnormal to have faith? Some people have their answer to that question ready. Faith, they will say, is a psychological aberration, a mental dysfunction. Sigmund Freud (1856-1939) was the most famous proponent of that view. He regarded religious belief as mere wishful thinking. But he also used less kind words, such as neurosis, illusion, poison, and intoxicant. The idea of God as the heavenly Father is just a projection, he argued, derived from our subconscious hang-ups about our human father.

Some scholars have pressed this suggestion even further. According to Michael P. Caroll, a Canadian professor of sociology, the praying of the rosary is a 'disguised gratification of repressed anal-erotic desires, a substitute for praying with one's faeces.' Warren Wilson (1874-1936), a Presbyterian church leader, blamed the growth of evangelical Protestantism in rural America on the fact that among country people there are many with inferior minds. Political scientist Herbert Simon (1916-2001) explained the behaviour of people like Mother Teresa, who are prepared to sacrifice their own interests to those of other people, in terms of 'docility' and 'bounded rationality.'

Well, Freud and others who thought and think like him are entitled to their opinion. For that's all it is: it is an *opinion*. There is not a scrap of real *evidence* to support this position. It should be noted that by putting it all in the realm of the subconscious Freud's theory is conveniently beyond any kind of verification. Moreover, the suggestion that faith can be reduced to wishful thinking has, upon a little reflection, not much to commend itself. For it is clear that many features of religious beliefs simply do not correspond to our wildest dreams, as the Christian philosopher Alvin Plantinga has so convincingly pointed out. Just think of concepts like sin and judgement! Many people actually do not like but very much *dis*like the idea of an omnipotent omniscient God who constantly monitors us and is going to judge us!

Even if an element of wishful thinking were involved, Plantinga argues, that may not actually discredit the notion of faith. Perhaps our Designer-God has constructed us with that kind of inbuilt desire, in order to help us to come to believe in him and become more aware of his presence. Maybe the great church father Augustine (354-430) was pointing us in the right direction with his famous dictum: Our hearts are restless till they rest in Thee, O God![22]

Before we leave this aspect, let me be clear that everything that parades as faith does not qualify as such. There is a kind of faith that is unwholesome and depresses people. It makes them feel boxed in and makes them neurotic or fearful. There is also the kind of faith that results in an obnoxious arrogance of having the final truth about everything, that stimulates intolerance and has often led to terrible persecution. Hans Küng (a Roman Catholic theologian who was, to put it mildly, not always appreciated by the leaders of his church) stated it very well:

'Belief in God was and is often authoritarian, tyrannical, and reactionary. It can produce anxiety, immaturity, narrow-mindedness, intolerance, injustice, frustration and social isolation; it can legitimize and inspire immorality, social abuse and wars within a nation and between nations. But belief in God can also be liberating, oriented on the future and beneficial to human beings; it can spread trust in life, maturity, broadmindedness, tolerance, solidarity, creative and social commitment; spiritual renewal, social reform and world peace.'[23]

'This 'liberating' and 'beneficial' kind of faith is the faith we will be discussing. Only the kind of faith that builds people, that makes them grow as individuals and makes them more human, is worthy of that name.'[24]

Faith is normal

Yes, some people talk about faith as if it is something strange and abnormal. We must vehemently protest against that notion. We all have faith in lots of things, all the time. When I drive my car across a narrow bridge, I do not hesitate to follow other cars across it. I do not stop and first launch a meticulous private investigation into the strength of the pillars underneath the bridge. The bridge has been there for many years. Hundreds of cars cross it every day. I have strong faith that it will also hold my car. We have faith in many other ways. I have never been to either the North Pole or the South Pole. But I have seen many pictures of people standing with their national flag on the point they say is the pole. I have no way of checking this. The pictures could have been faked in Northern Canada or Siberia or by a clever computer whiz-kid in Miami. But I believe that the world is a globe and that there are two points at opposite sides which we call the poles, and I do not doubt that by now there have been quite a few people who have managed to get there by various means. Likewise, when we take the bus or get on a plane, we have faith in the skills of the driver or the pilot, and when we go to a restaurant we have faith that the cook will not poison us.

There are other ways in which most people show faith. Normally we believe what people say. There may be some persons whom we have learned to approach with a fair amount of scepticism as to the trustworthiness of what they tell us, but the world would stop functioning if, in general, we could no longer believe what people say. And we are familiar with yet another kind of faith. People believe in the causes they support and in the assignments to which they dedicate their time. They believe that certain things are worthy of their attention while other things are not.

Many of us, fortunately, also believe in people in a more fundamental sense than just trusting in some of their skills and trusting in what they tell us. We believe in them as persons. We believe in their integrity, and we somehow know, deep down, that they are good people who deserve our admiration and loyalty.

Yet, when discussing religious faith, we need to take the definition of 'faith' quite a bit further. Let me offer two definitions. One is from the German-born American theologian-philosopher J. P. Tillich, who wrote extensively on the relationship between religion and psychology. He defined religious faith as follows: 'Faith is the state of being ultimately concerned: the dynamics of faith are the dynamics of man's ultimate concern.'[25] It seems a bit philosophical but a better description would be hard to find. Yet maybe there is a still better definition, which has been provided by the writer of one of the 'books' of the Bible. It is, in fact, the only straightforward definition of faith that can be found in the entire Bible. This author suggests the following description: 'Faith is being sure of what we hope for, and certain of what we do not see.'[26]

These two definitions have one main characteristic in common. They do not define faith by first referring to some intellectual arguments. Faith, it appears, does not – at least not primarily – result from the intellectual acceptance of certain logical arguments or certain indubitable propositions, or even from the content of a string of 'justifiable beliefs'. Faith, both definitions tell us, is a certainty of a different kind. It goes beyond what we can argue with our minds, however brilliant we may think we are, and it goes beyond any kind of normal sense-perception. We are certain, not of what we see – after all: what we see might be appearance rather reality – but of things we do *not* see! Whatever else religious faith may be, it has to do with a reality, with a certainty about unseen things that concern us in an existential, ultimate way.

This assertion seems to make us immediately vulnerable to the critic who will accuse the person who is willing to define faith along these terms as having said 'goodbye' to reason and intelligence. They will remind us of what Mark Twain once said: Faith is believing what you know ain't true!

The sceptics and the agnostics will, of course, argue that faith must be based on solid evidence, which can be empirically verified, i.e. on proof that can be checked by the use of our senses. (However, you need to be aware of a fatal inconsistency in the actions and the reasoning of the sceptic: The sceptic who believes she cannot be sure of anything, invariably leaves her scepticism behind in concrete situations. When her house is on fire she will not doubt the reality of the fire but call the emergency number, grab a few valuables and get out of the house. Also, it is important to realize that the sceptic is utterly inconsistent even in her philosophical argumentation; she relies on her mental faculties to conclude that these faculties are unreliable!)

Naturally, reason is important and faith is not to be confused with mere *fideism*, i.e. with a belief that simply decides to believe, without any reference to the 'web' of at least a number of 'justifiable beliefs' (see previous chapter). But when push comes to shove, what solid reason do we have to trust one particular faculty with which we have been endowed more than other faculties we are equipped with? Why should we, for instance, trust reason more than perception? Or intuition, for that matter? To choose to do so is, when everything is said and done, an arbitrary decision.[27]

Let us be clear about what faith is *not*. It is not, on the one hand, mere intellectual assent to a number of philosophical or theological propositions. On the other hand, it is not a matter of leaving our intellect behind and a willingness to enter a world of magic or science-fiction in which everything is possible. Allow me to refer at some length to some of the thoughts of Hans Küng.[28] Faith, Küng says, 'would be half a thing were it only to address our understanding and reason and not the whole person, including our hearts.' It is not primarily a matter of theological statements or doctrines as defined by a church, or intellectual arguments and rational discourse, but has much to do also with our imagination and emotions.

When we say that we believe in God we do not claim that we know exactly who and what God is. 'God is by definition that which cannot be defined, that which cannot be limited: a literally invisible, unfathomable, incomprehensible, infinite reality.' The existence of God is for many who have given the matter serious thought a 'justifiable belief,' but, as we saw earlier, God's existence can never be demonstrated with finality by logical argument or scientific experiment. Just as, Küng hastens to add, so far no one has produced a convincing proof for the non-existence of God either. Believing in God is an act of the human person as a whole, of reason and heart; an 'act of reasonable trust for which there may not be strict proofs, but for which there are good reasons. . . . So it is not just a matter of holding statements to be true, but a commitment of the whole person, not primarily to specific statements, but to the very reality of God.'

One point is of such decisive importance that it cannot be overemphasized. Christian faith has first of all to do with trust in a 'person'. Some mistakenly centre their faith on the Bible. Many Protestant Christians have made that error. Many of them worship a book rather than a Person; they place their faith in a document rather than in the One to whom the document refers. Many Roman Catholics commit the mistake of making their church the focus of their faith, rather than the One the church has been called to proclaim. Many believers in orthodox denominations tend to confuse faith with tradition and forget that faith concerns the One whom tradition hands down to us.[29] Faith is a person-to-Person relationship. Everything else is secondary.

How to get faith if you want it

But back to the question where and how faith originates. Can you simply choose to have faith? Or not to have it? Are some people born with a special capacity to have faith? Is it mainly a matter of environment and upbringing? Why is it that some people would like to get away from their faith and do not succeed in casting it off, while others say they envy people who have faith, but claim they do not know how to obtain such faith for themselves? Those are far from simple questions. But try to suspend judgement for a while, as I provide a rough sketch of the answer that is provided in the Bible, and by some who have read the Bible and have drawn a few conclusions from what they have read. It runs as follows: God has designed us with a capacity for faith. There is something in us that recognizes that he is there and wants to reach out to us – that he wants to commune with us. Call it a sixth or seventh sense, or give it a Latin name, as the sixteenth century church reformer John Calvin did[30] – or describe it as an inner certainty that there is a God who not only exists, but who cares – whatever you call it, it is there.

Unfortunately, this sense appears to be weakened in many of

us or to be even totally obliterated in some of us. Why is this? The reason for this is that something has gone wrong with humanity. The biblical word for what happened is 'sin'. We will return to this later, in chapter five, in more detail. But in this connection we must mention it in a preliminary way. You may have heard Christians talk about 'original' sin. When they use this term they do not use it in the sense that some sins are so special and unique that they might be called 'original', meaning that they are the result of an individual's creativity or ability to do something bad in a way no one else has as yet thought of. No, the term 'original sin' refers to the idea that something has, at some point in the past, gone wrong with the human race, and that ever since human beings have had some inborn handicaps. We often have the tendency to do what our conscience tells us is wrong. (Most of us will acknowledge that there is some inner 'voice' which with greater or lesser clarity tells us there is a difference between right and wrong and good and evil; this is what we call our 'conscience'.) A passage in the Bible states the tragic reality very succinctly: 'I do not understand what I do. For what I want to do I do not do, but what I hate I do.'[31] G. K. Chesterton (1874-1936), the well-known author who later in life converted to Christianity, once remarked that if there is any theological concept that can be empirically verified it is the reality of 'original sin.' It has, he says, tragically enough been verified in wars, cruelty and hatefulness throughout history.[32] The tragic consequence of what went wrong is that the human opposition against God (another way of describing 'sin') seems to have affected the human ability to 'commune' with him; it has negatively impacted upon this faculty with which God equipped the creature he had designed. No longer were God and man, as it were, on the same wave length, nor – and that may well be the crucial issue – have many men and women been using this capacity as eagerly and intensely as God had intended.

As people got into the habit of not staying attuned to a sense of a divine presence, their antenna for this divine signal became rusty. Many, in fact, have never learned to use it and to direct their antenna to the Source of the signal. Receiving this signal from our Designer-God and responding to it, therefore remained something unknown and foreign to their world. Plantinga argues that this 'natural knowledge of God' has been 'weakened, reduced, overlaid, or impeded by sin and its consequences'. The 'sense of the divine' has, as a result, been narrowed in scope and partially suppressed. And he goes on to argue that it is far more reasonable to argue that lack or absence of faith is therefore a dysfunction or even a disease, than to say with Marx and his followers that faith is a mental dysfunction or a dangerous opiate which leads to tragic addiction.[33]

H. C. Rümke (1893-1967), one of the most prominent Dutch psychiatrists of the twentieth century, made a strong case for the normality of religious belief in his classic book about character and disposition in relationship to belief and unbelief.[34] He affirms what we already stated above. If we define faith as trusting somthing to be true, and as acting on that trust, without final intellectual evidence, we must conclude, he says, that there are no people who do not have faith. Our entire existence is based on that kind of trusting faith which is not unlike instinct or intuition. Every human being has faith in many areas of life. Religious belief is a particular form of faith. To suggest that this kind of faith is evidence of mental dysfunction or a lack of maturity shows an unreasonable bias.[35]

The capacity to receive and give love is rather similar, I think, to the capacity for religious belief. For most people love is something natural. From the first moments of their lives, even before they can walk and talk, they are able to respond to the love-signals of the mother. We are at a loss to explain this astounding love-mechanism. But it is there. Unless there is some personality disorder, or unless something goes terribly wrong in our childhood years, we grow up with this mysterious capacity to recognize love, to receive and to give it. Love, we might say, is a gift we have been given. It does not depend on intellectual arguments, even though we know we should not love without using our brain. There are degrees in the capacity of people to give and receive love, however. Some people no longer seem to have the antenna for receiving signals of love from others and somehow are unable to respond to such signals. But this does not lead us to doubt the reality and normality of love.

Faith – the capacity to believe and trust in God utterly, and the intense desire to know more about him and to learn what he wants for us and from us – is also a gift. All people have received the gift to a greater or lesser degree. Paul, a biblical author who wrote a series of letters to some of the mid-first century Christian churches, suggests that God has from the very beginning implanted some basic knowledge about himself in the minds of all people. He points specifically to nature as a source of awareness of God, when he states, 'For since the creation of the world God's invisible qualities – his eternal power and divine nature – have been clearly seen, being understood from what has been made, so that men are without excuse.'[36] This awareness of the divine does not come as the result of deep thinking or the reading of sophisticated philosophical books or even through a diligent reading of the Bible, though all these things have their place. It is a gift that just comes to us. The same author we have quoted wrote to another local church about the concepts of grace and faith and referred to these as a gift from God.[37] Surely, if our reasoning thus far has been 'justified', we are also more than 'justified' to believe that the Designer-God made us with an in-built capacity to react to signals about his existence, presence and involvement with us.

Faith in God does not primarily result from convincing arguments. People who have come to believe will tell you different stories as to how they acquired their faith. Some will say that, deep down, it has always been there. Others will be able to pinpoint a precise moment from which they first experienced faith. Still others cannot exactly tell you how they came to believe. But people who talk to you about the history of their faith do not usually refer to intellectual arguments, although these may have provided further depth to their faith. When pointing to when and where it started, they almost talk in a language of sense perception. They say they *felt* a divine presence; they were overwhelmed by *looking* at the multitude of stars during a clear night. They speak in terms of awe, of being *touched* in their innermost self. They suddenly felt they should pray and felt that their prayers were *heard*. There is no doubt that faith has a strong experiential component. It reaches into our mind, but certainly also into our affections.

But let's make no mistake: Faith may not primarily start from reflection but, once it is there, it will lead most assuredly to reflection. If you become aware of the Someone we call God, and sense a fundamental dependence on this Someone, a deep inner trust of this Someone, you will realize that this trust can only grow as you acquire further knowledge about this Someone. Faith is not just feeling, but also has structure and content. Yet Adventist theologian Fritz Guy is absolutely right when he states that the 'content of the faith is existentially only significant in connection with a response of trust; it is the content of personal belief.'[38]

And what of the volitional aspect (the matter of our will)? Can we *decide* that we will have faith or can we *refuse* to have faith? Can we decide what package of propositions we want to believe in and what elements of the Christians teachings we will disregard? Let me quote Rümke again:

'I have never been able to observe a case in which someone found faith through thinking or willing. When we look at those who say that they have been brought to faith by rational argument, we always find that the term "rational" has to be taken in a very loose sense. In further discussions they will often agree that the thought process contained several links which are identical with believing trust.

'In studying those who say that they have acquired faith through their will, I have often discovered that their faith was not genuine, or that this will to believe was, in actual fact, already a form of faith that had somehow developed.

'I cannot say that it is absolutely impossible that there are cases where reason and will have led to faith. I can only say that I have never encountered such cases. But I do think that "thinking" and "willing" can play an important role in the inner processing of our experience and in the place we attribute to religion.'[39]

Let me pull some of the things together that we talked about so far. I have suggested in chapter one that faith in a Designer God is at least a 'justifiable' belief, in particular in view of the fact that so many people throughout time and in all cultures have had a deep sense of ultimate dependence on Something or Someone far beyond their own private or social world. And in chapter two we have pursued the question of truth and have concluded (and I hope you have been able to come along in that conclusion) that the idea of truth is still tenable, even in our postmodern era in which *absolute truth* is considered with great suspicion), and that it is not unreasonable to assume that, if there is a Designer-God, he may well have designed us with a capacity and opportunity for acquiring some true knowledge about him. We have briefly looked at the role of the Bible in that respect. And yet in this chapter we arrived at the point where we said that acknowledgment of this 'justifiable' belief in a Designer-God, which provides our existence with meaning, and the possibility of finding truth about him, does not lead automatically to genuine religious faith. And so far, we have seen in this chapter that those who do not have faith in God are expected to assume quite a few things in this process of acquiring faith. Complicated religious concepts have been mentioned: the sense of divine awareness that has been weakened or distorted by 'sin' and the kindling or rekindling of faith as a 'gift' from God.

Does all of this not require a number of giant steps? Yes, but isn't that inherent in discovery and adventure? And, surely, this is not a blind leap in the dark over an abyss of totally unknown width. The kinds of things we are asked to believe are not at all like the things we encounter in the world of Asimov or Harry Potter. They may not be open to sense verification or laboratory inspection, but they are part of a web of 'justifiable beliefs' and fit together in a coherent story.

How do you take this leap? Or, to use the other metaphor: Where do you go to get the 'gift' of faith? I cannot propose a twelve-point programme that will help you move from unbelief to belief. It does not work that way. It seems reasonable that if there is a Designer-God who designed us with the capacity for faith, he would be more than prepared to give the gift of faith to those who have somehow lost it. But might he also sometimes wait and do so only when he feels the occasion is right? Or when he feels the intended receiver has the right attitude, the openness and appreciation for the gift?

If something is a free gift, there is nothing you can do to earn it. But it may be possible to frequent the places where such a gift is likely to be handed out. If you want to declare your love to another person, you will hardly do so while waiting your turn in the check-out line of the supermarket, or when you see how the target of your love is totally exhausted after a frustrating day at the office. Romance usually demands a particular kind of setting. A candlelight dinner, a summer evening river cruise or a walk along a quiet beach will greatly enhance the chances of success when seeking to communicate your love. Similarly, people have found faith in all kinds of circumstances, but aspects of time and place often play a major role. The atmosphere of a medieval cathedral, the reading of a spiritual book, a piece of music, the company of a partner or a good friend who is a genuine believer, being captivated by the beauty of nature – all of these may create the environment in which this *sensus divinatis*, this feeling of ultimate dependence, this certainty that there is One who cares, may get a better chance than in the hustle and bustle of the office or the morning rush hour. Above anything else we must remember that faith requires expectation and openness. We must hold out our hand if we want to receive the gift. We must be willing to step forward, and take the leap.

And we must pray. But I can hear the immediate objection: 'Prayer does not precede faith but follows faith. Believers pray. Unbelievers do not pray.' In a sense that is correct. Those who have faith in God want to talk to the One in whom they believe. But, at the same time, it is also true that prayer may lead to faith. If there is this God who wants us to have faith, would he not have an open ear for even the most primitive of prayers that says: Please, God, whoever you are, give me that gift?

The 'stuff' of belief

Faith is trust. Faith is a relationship. But faith also has propositional content. It is in many ways like a relationship between people who are close to each other. When you feel you have met your mate for life, you are in love. Gradually a true and deepening relationship develops and you want to know everything about the person you love. About her background and her family. But especially also about who she really is: What does she like or dislike? What are her tastes? What are her ideals? Her hobbies? And, what will she expect from you? Are you able to be and to provide what she would like you to be and to give? Naturally, believers in God also want to know more about him – about who he is and what he does, and what he would expect from us as partners in a relationship.

The systematic enquiry into who and what God is and does is called *theology*. And the statements which summarize the conclusions of the theologians are referred to as doctrines. The term creed (derived from the Latin *credo*=I believe) is reserved for official doctrinal statements which are shared by most Christian churches and for the specific official 'confessional' statements of individual churches or denominations.

Very often these creeds or doctrinal statements have such immense authority, that it has become almost impossible to change even a sentence or a single word. Of course, they are the product of long and intense corporate reflection and, therefore, deserve to be regarded with respect. But we should never forget that, in final analysis, such creedal statements are human formulas. They inevitably use words which were intelligible and common at the time when they were first formulated, but may be rather foggy for readers in our time, in particular if these readers have no religious background. Naturally they reflect the philosophies of the time in which they were adopted. Also, these formulations make judgements about what is of greater and of lesser importance, and current thinking may not always agree with that centuries-old judgement. Some churches say they refuse to be bound by creeds or other formal statements of belief, but in actual reality most of these have found it difficult to withstand the internal pressure of their members to define where the church stands on various theological issues.

I am convinced that a community of faith needs to arrive at a consensus about what they see as the core content of the Christian faith, even though I want to add immediately that any such statement must always be provisional and may from time to time have to be updated. The times change and the way we understand and apply the biblical revelation changes with the times. Doctrines and summaries of the content of the faith are needed. They may be compared to the function of grammar.

Language cannot be reduced to grammar. When we speak or write, we want to communicate a certain message. The content of the sender's message must be received and understood by the receiver. There will be very little, if any, communication, however, if words are just lumped together without a deliberate structure. The message will simply not be received.

The rules of grammar provide structure to our language; they help communicate the message but they are not to be confused with the message itself. The comparison may not apply in every aspect, but nonetheless helps to explain the role of doctrine. It is important to note that faith is more than a matter of creedal statements and doctrines. But faith seeks to understand itself, as the famous medieval Anselm (c. 1033-1109) pointed out. And in order to do so, it needs to formulate certain concepts and 'teachings'. The doctrines assist us in talking about God and discovering ever more depth in God's revelation to us, and in organizing our insights and the implications thereof.

Not all doctrines are equally important. It has been suggested by Robert C. Greer in his book on Christian options in our postmodern era that we may distinguish different levels of doctrinal statements.[40] First, there are some basic doctrines which most Christian churches have in common, such as for instance those that are listed in the Apostolic Creed, a document which dates from the third century AD and summarizes a few key concepts with regard to God, Jesus, the Holy Spirit, salvation, future life and the church. Then, there are doctrines which are not universally shared but are part of the religious heritage of particular denominations (such as baptism by immersion or the weekly day of rest). Finally, there is a deposit of community thinking about all kinds of religious and ethical issues that has become significant for the members of a particular faith community. This latter category does, however, not belong to the core doctrines of a denomination, and there may well be considerable difference of opinion among the members about these ideas. In this book we will deal to some extent with the first two levels of doctrine. I will touch upon the main 'general' Christian doctrines and upon the most significant doctrines of the Seventh-day Adventist Church – the community to which I belong. I will not do this in the order in which these teachings are listed in any of the traditional Christian Creeds or in any document of my own church, but will refer to them when they fit logically into our ten-step discovery journey.

For now, take the leap of faith. Open your inner self to the possibility of faith in the One who has designed you. And, if you have not done so before, begin to talk to him and to others who have found faith. If someone invites you to come to their church or to some other place where people 'exercise' their faith, simply try it. What have you got to lose? And start reading a modern language version of the Bible. Do not give up too easily. Faith is a gift. But stretch out to receive it. And you will find that faith is not just 'for dummies'. I quote Alvin Plantinga once more and let him say what I would want to underline at the end of this chapter:

'My aim is to show how it can be that Christians can be justified, rational . . . and warranted in holding full-blooded Christian belief – not just ignorant fundamentalists, but sophisticated, aware, educated, turn-of-the millennium people, who have read Freud and Nietzsche, their Hume and their Mackie, their Dennet and Dawkins.'[41]

It may take some time before your faith has fully replaced your former unbelief and present doubt. If so, repeat the words of a man who once came to Jesus and prayed this simple prayer: 'I do believe; help me overcome my unbelief!'[42]

Chapter four

Hope

What is life without hope? What real meaning can there be, even if there is a God, but if there is no hope for the future in this life and no hope for a life beyond this life? It may not seem so bad for those who have more than they need, and who are healthy and successful. For most of us, however, life has its ups and downs, and for many it unfortunately has rather fewer ups than downs. Without hope life quickly deteriorates into a miserable existence.

The concept of hope is closely tied to meaning and faith. Hope reinforces the meaning of life. It inspires and enables us to remain positive and proactive. It helps us to keep our eyes fixed on our goals, to find the buoyancy to live with purpose and to seize our full potential. Faith and hope are not fully synonymous but they are closely linked. To have faith means to have hope.

Why do we dare to hope? This is how Christians will answer that question: Because we believe in a God who has designed us and made us, who wants to communicate with us, and who wants to care for us. They will say, we have hope *because there is a God who loves us.* Faith, hope and love are concepts which are inseparably connected. Nowhere is this more clearly articulated than in a famous Bible chapter which I recommend everyone to read and re-read regularly: the thirteenth chapter of the first letter written by the apostle Paul to the church in the Greek city of Corinth. He gives an in-depth description of the true character of love – a description which is as challenging now as it was when he wrote the words. At the end of this superb passage he concludes that there are three key concepts in the life of the Christian: faith, hope and love. But love is even more important, he says, than faith and hope.[43]

Why then start with *faith* (chapter three) and continue with *hope* (this chapter), rather than begin with *love*? Admittedly, I could have taken another approach. But I believe the order in which I deal with these three concepts has much to commend itself. For faith leads to hope; hope builds on it and derives its credibility from it. Yet we must also immediately point to God's love. We can have hope as soon as we have found reason to believe in God. What we continue to discover about him gives us ever increasing hope. It is in particular the ongoing discovery of God's infinite love (see chapter five) which anchors our hope. We might therefore summarize this chapter in just a few words: *There is hope for those who have faith in a God who loves us*.

Hopelessness versus hope

We must briefly return to a criticism which we encountered when we talked about the reality of faith. Faith, some argue in their Freudian misconception, is wishful thinking. They maintain that hope (at least in its true, undiluted, Christian sense) is like faith: it is just pie in the sky, and no more than illusion. It may fool many people, especially those who are at the bottom of the social ladder and who need this dreamlike illusion to keep going, but that does not give it any credence! The focus on a hereafter, they say, discourages involvement with the world of the here and now.

Again, the answer to that kind of criticism would be: this is merely a matter of opinion. The critics cannot prove that the Christian's hope is just pious words without any corresponding substance. But the believer, on the other hand, can convincingly argue that the various 'justifiable beliefs' all fit together coherently in a finely woven web of truth, once you have ventured out to take the leap of faith. And who will deny that hope is what millions of people in today's world desperately need?

Hope has been at a low ebb since '9/11'. What hope is there for a peaceful future if terrorists can bring sudden death and instant destruction in trains, buses and theatres, and can fly commercial airliners into office skyscrapers? What hope is there in countries where brutal civil wars have brought decades of death and destruction and where the value of a human life has been discounted to almost nothing? What hope is there if repeated seasons of drought and clouds of locusts, which every single day eat the equivalent of several times their own body weight, bring famine to large areas in sub-Saharan Africa? What hope is there for the millions of HIV and AIDS victims in the developing world? And for all those whose lives are wasting away in detention centres? What hope is there for those who suffer from Altzheimer's disease or other physically or mentally debilitating illnesses? What is there for those who have lost their loved ones in a plane crash or in a tidal wave? What hope is left for people who have just seen their marriage go on the rocks and who are desperate because they have lost their children to the drug scene or worse?

Life may not be too bad for many of us who live in a developed-world setting, and who happen to be healthy, are in a good relationship and have a promising career. Life may not be too bad for the privileged elite or even the small middle-class in a number of developing countries. But the majority of this world's inhabitants are not so fortunate. Some two billion people live under the poverty line. Hundreds of millions of adult men and women cannot read or write. And the average life expectancy worldwide is some thirty years below the life expectancy in the Western world. The reality is that most people in today's world have little reason to be hopeful. Many lead a life that is characterized by fear and despair. This stark reality reminds me of a prediction which we find in the New Testament (the second major section of the Bible) where we are told that there will come a time that people will 'faint from terror' as they see the terrible things that happen around them.[44] These words certainly seem to apply to the dismal situation hundreds of millions of people are facing today.

However, in contrast with this picture of gloom and dismay, there is hope. Christians, a biblical passage tells us, are not like people who live without hope.[45] That is the defining difference between those who have faith in God and those who don't: hope instead of hopelessness. Hope for each of us individually and hope for Planet Earth. However, we must define hope in the proper way. Hope in the biblical sense is not synonymous with unrealistic daydreaming or a matter of just striking it lucky. When we hope to win a million dollars in the state lottery or hope to take first prize in a local beauty contest, we are talking about something that has nothing to do with the hope of the Christian faith.

What people call hope and refer to as progress is often simply characterized by materialistic desire. They hope the FTSE 500, the Dow Jones and the NASDAQ will continue to climb. They hope their disposable income will continue to grow and the value of their house will steadily increase. They hope that, next year, they will be able to buy or lease a larger and fancier car. Fortunately, not everybody colours his hope in such materialistic shades. Some also genuinely hope that the chasm between rich and poor will gradually close; that the wars in Africa will stop; that more people all over the world will succeed in adopting a healthier lifestyle; that mankind will do all it can to protect nature; that the rich countries will provide the resources to stop world hunger and widespread illiteracy. Yet this is still a far cry from the hope of the Christian faith.

We must also be clear that hope is not to be confused with optimism. I like people who are optimistic. I tend to be an optimist myself. But I often pay for it dearly, when I have made my decisions on the basis of best-case scenarios and have been too generous when estimating income and unrealistic when estimating expense. Rudolph W. Giuliani, the mayor of New York at the time of '9/11', wrote a book about his leadership principles. One of them is: Underpromise and Overdeliver.[46] He had learned his lessons about the risks of too much optimism! One can easily be trapped in a cycle of unrealistic expectations. The crucial difference between optimism and hope is that optimism is based on what I see, or imagine that I see, while the Christian hope is – like faith – based on a reality which I do not see. The Bible puts it like this: 'Hope that is seen is no hope at all. Who hopes for what he already has?'[47]

Optimism and belief in progress is primarily based on human achievement. It was a prominent aspect of 'modern' Enlightenment thinking which saw no limit to what might be achieved. Human technology would, in a Jules Vernes-like fashion, overcome the limitations of travel and communication; new medicines would halt murderous diseases like the Spanish Influenza and smallpox. New machines would deliver us from tedious routine and more wealth would make life for all more pleasurable. In our postmodern era we have at last concluded that this optimism is largely misplaced. The world has not become the peaceful and prosperous paradise that was envisaged. The reality is that we have not mastered nature but have largely destroyed it. We have not cared for the earth but have exploited its resources in a shortsighted and selfish way. We have not become one great happy human family, but have created wellnigh unbridgeable tensions between the haves and the havenots, between the North and the South, between Christians and Muslims, and between white and black. The bleak reality of this world provides little reason for optimism. But in spite of this there is hope.

Why can we hope in spite of the mess we often make in our own lives and the corporate mess we have managed to create in this world? Our hope is not based on technology. I would not want to do without many of the things that have resulted from our technological inventions and developments. I am happy that I can write on a laptop and have convenient software, and I appreciate that I have a satellite dish on the roof of my garage which enables me to watch hundreds of local and national channels, as well as CNN and Sky-news. But technology is not the final answer to today's problems. For advanced technology has also resulted in smart bombs and surgical air strikes. It also enables the terrorists to play their deadly games with innocent lives.

True hope that deserves the name is not built on the work of politicians, either, or on the efforts of the UN or the European Union. We need politicians with integrity and courage, and we need international organizations that have the guts and the means to bring peace to the war-torn areas of our globe. But if history has taught us anything it should at least have made it clear to us that politics are often a major part of the problem rather than of the solution.

Nor can hope be based on a belief in evolution. Even if the evolutionary theory were true, it would be such a slow process that I would find little personal hope in it. Even if evolution could be proven, it would provide little ground for real hope with its basic premise of a relentless and wasteful struggle for survival, resulting only in the survival of a few of the very fittest.

The basis of hope

The hope of the Christian faith has several dimensions. It has to do with the individual person, but it also extends to the entire human race. It has to do with the here and now of this world, but also with the future, even beyond the grave. It determines how we view ourselves and the people around us, and how we view the world. What is the basis for such a far-reaching hope? It must be some momentous fact or event which allows us to have this hope. What is it?

The short answer to this question is encapsulated in just three words: *God loves us*. The longer answer that will be developed in the next few pages will expand on that kernel of absolute truth. This is the basis for every other doctrinal or theological statement. This is the core of it all. Take this conviction away, and there is no Christian faith and no hope.

Christian hope is anchored in God and his love for men and women like you and me.

This brings us to the question to which we have already alluded several times. What is our Designer-God like? What is his nature? That is, what is his character? After having studied the biblical text and having analyzed all the direct and indirect qualifications of God, theologians have come up with a number of terms to describe the indescribable. God is, they say, all-powerful or omnipotent. That is to say, because he is God he can do anything he wants to do. (Of course, that statement must be qualified: he can do everything that is consistent with his nature.) God is also omniscient. That means that, being God, he knows everything there is to know and there is nothing anyone can keep a secret from him. He is also omnipresent. For, being God, he cannot be bound to one particular location as we are. Distance is no problem to him. God is, theologians say, eternal and infinite. That is, he has always existed and will always exist. And whatever we say about him, there always remains more to say, for he is beyond anything we can imagine. When Moses, a leader of the people of Israel some 1400 years BC, wanted to know the name of God, he received a puzzling response, yet one that said it all. God called himself the 'I AM'.[48] This means that God is everything he is in a totally complete, infinite way. We are searching for words and we know they are inadequate. For what do we, who may live to be 80 or 90, know about eternity? What do we, who are so painfully limited in our skills and possibilities, know about being all-mighty? What do utterly finite beings know about being infinite? Human words and concepts will never suffice when we try to describe God. But they help us to catch a glimpse of the truth of what God is.

Other words are suggested to describe God's character. He is patient and full of understanding. God is righteous and impartial, but at the same time he is full of grace and mercy. He is, in one word, a God of *love*. The best known text in the entire Bible underlines the essence of the divine: *God is love*.[49]

In a way, it all seems very simple. It is, indeed, but at the same time these concepts are mind-boggling and can serve as the theme for life-long meditation, because they have tremendous implications. For (and here I need to quote from the Bible again), 'God so loved the world' (me, you, everybody) 'that he sent his Son' (Jesus Christ) into this world for a very specific purpose. His Son was to be the instrument to restore the relationship between us and God.[50] Let's see what this means (and whether our initial leap of faith may have to be followed by some further leaps).

Things went wrong. The human beings God had so carefully

designed, made a dramatic move away from him. They rebelled and the biblical story tells us that, as a result, everything in this world was affected. Disease and death were introduced, war and cruelty made their entry. Gradually, the desire and capacity to get in touch with the divine was seriously impaired. How did this all happen? Search the Bible for the rest of your life and think about it till you fall off your chair from exhaustion, but you will never understand what exactly happened. It exceeds our human understanding. Yet we see the terrible reality of evil and wrongdoing all around us. Behind the symbolism that some of the Bible writers used we learn that, although mankind must take the responsibility for what went wrong, there was a supra-human dimension – Evil with a capital letter – involved. The biblical name for the original instigator of evil is Satan.[51] And, if it is true that there is a supernatural dimension to evil, it stands to reason that the solution for this unparalleled predicament must also come from a supernatural source. Experience has amply shown that mankind cannot pull itself up by its corporate bootstraps to escape from the quicksand of global misery and misconduct.

It belongs to the very core of the Christian message (the Greek word for 'gospel' is literally: the 'good news') that a solution has been provided. Jesus Christ, the Son of God, came to this earth some 2,000 years ago, in a human body and at a concrete location, and became the Solution for the sin problem. He lived a perfect life but annoyed the religious and political establishment to the point that they sought to eliminate him. Eventually he was executed on a cross and died. His death, the Christian says, was not a punishment for anything he himself did. It somehow 'atoned' for the sins of us all. And the good news goes on. After he was laid in a tomb, he rose from death on the third day and then, forty days later, 'ascended' into heaven. And the good news continues even further. For he did not remain idle after his return to heaven, but is still intimately involved with the affairs of men. And he will come to this world a second time. Some time soon. His second coming will bring revolutionary change. This world will be exchanged for a world which is perfect, populated by those who have been 'saved' after they made the conscious choice to believe in God. Then eternity begins.

Surely, if all this is true, there is indeed ample reason to hope. I believe this *is* true. All of this is included in the leap of faith I invite you to make if you have not already done so. I do not expect you to grasp immediately all the aspects of the previous two paragraphs. I have studied theology for over forty years and I have read the Bible many times and have also read many hundreds of theological books, and I must confess that there continue to be many questions in my own mind as to how I must understand certain elements of this 'good news'. As stated earlier, we must realize that our human vocabulary is extremely limited and words do not begin to give complete descriptions of the concepts we are dealing with. When we apply such words as 'person' and 'personality' to God, we do so because those are the only words we happen to have to speak about the being of God. 'Personality' is the very least we want to attribute to God. God is more than we are, and 'personality' – but then in more perfect and infinite form – is therefore the very least we would want to ascribe to him. When we follow the biblical language and call Jesus the 'Son' of God the 'Father', we do not intend to imply any biological relationship or gender specification. The words are used because they help us to catch a glimpse of the closeness of the relationship between the 'members' of the Godhead.

When we refer to 'heaven' we are not quite sure what we refer to. Is it a location in outer space where God 'lives'? That may be too simplistic a notion as God is also described as the Spirit[52] who is everywhere. (The placing of so many words between quotation marks is intentional. It indicates that these words are not being used in their common everyday sense, but are employed because of the limitations of human language when referring to the realm of the divine. But that does not mean that they are without communicative value. They do help us to learn enough about God to relate to him in a meaningful way.)

There is enough historical evidence for the fact that a remarkable Jewish rabbi with the name Jesus did indeed live in Palestine in the first few decades of the Christian era. But there is, of course, no historical corroboration for the biblical story of the manner of his birth: we are told that a young woman named

Mary became pregnant without having had sex! For many, this idea of a 'virgin birth' is totally preposterous. And, admittedly, many theological scholars also consider this story merely a pious myth. I am also puzzled how something so exceptional could have happened, but am satisfied with the thought that we would *expect* something completely out of the ordinary to occur when divinity decides to come down to the level of humanity. Is it too much to expect something that is totally unique and extraordinary when God comes to live among us for some thirty-three years in the person of Jesus Christ?

The historical evidence for the fact that this Jesus died and then, after three days, came back from death, is largely circumstantial, but nonetheless impressive. Normally, movements quickly disintegrate when the leader has come to an ignominious end. If the death of Jesus at the hands of his Roman torturers had been the end of his life's story, there would not have been much of a Jesus movement for very long. It would have fizzled out within years at the most. But, apparently, something totally unexpected happened, which changed the mood of the small group of prospective leaders of the Jesus movement from dejection and total frustration into one of courageous energy and lifelong involvement with an ever growing, internationally expanding movement. The existence and spectacular growth of the early Christian church is inexplicable without some momentous event. That event, Christians have always maintained, was the miracle of the resurrection of Jesus Christ. People who knew he had died, had seen convincing proof of his resurrection, and from this they derived the faith and the courage to go out into the world to preach their message of hope.

In the next chapter I will speak in more detail about the deeper meaning of Jesus' death and return to life, and specifically about the question why he died. The point I want to underline here is that the hope of the Christian is based on some extraordinary things. *If we can trust the 'goods news' of the Bible and can believe that these things, however strange and miraculous, are true, our hope has a firm basis indeed.*

Hope for each individual

It is important to connect all this with the biblical view of man. While we are reminded that there is something fundamentally wrong with us because of the sin phenomenon, this picture is balanced by several statements in the Bible which remind us that men and women have originally been designed to have a status almost on a par with that of angels,[53] and that we have been created in 'the image of God'.[54] This is not to suggest that we outwardly look like God, or that God has a physical body which is similar in appearance to our body. We would seriously cheapen God's infinity if we were to bring him down to our physical level. The term 'image of God' rather suggests that we have capabilities which resemble (on our level) some of the capabilities which God has on his level. I wonder whether it has, most of all, to do with the fact that God, as the Creator-Designer, has made us with the gift of creativity, with the ability to communicate, and with the capability to establish a love relationship with others.

In several passages in the New Testament we find a clear message that, in addition, we all have certain 'talents'. There is no person who has no talent at all.[55] There is often a tendency to regard certain people as utterly hopeless cases. We are inclined to write them off as we see no chance for improvement. We see no redeeming features and give up on them. That, however, is not the Christian way of looking at people. Everybody has something positive, for each human being still bears something of the 'image of God', and everybody has some gift. And there is more. There is always some potential for acquiring further skills and for further learning and personal growth. There is, therefore, always hope, and no human being should be classified as hopeless. But there is still more. There may be things we cannot change about ourselves, in particular with regard to our exterior. But a fundamental change of attitude, an 'extreme makeover' of behaviour, of perspective and inner motivation, is possible. *For everyone*. That is part of the hope of the Christian. A person can find the desire and inner strength to turn around and make a fundamentally new start. The technical biblical term for this process is 'conversion'. The pathway is faith in God, communication with

God, a personal decision to change and to seek the power to do so, and to persevere. It may seem rather unlikely to some, but millions can testify that, somehow, for them this has actually worked! The direction of their lives has changed. From self-centred callous people they have been transformed into warm, loving persons. They have been able to overcome addictions and disagreeable habits. They no longer need the party scene to fill their weekends. They find pleasure and satisfaction in the small joys of life, and have found purpose in life where earlier they felt they had nothing to live for.

That is what people who have faith in God and in his power may hope for. Of course, we can change some things by the power of our will. We can pledge on New Year's Eve that we will stop smoking or begin with a serious diet. And we may succeed. But the total change that can come when we redirect our lives is of a different order. In biblical language it is referred to as 'a new heart' – not a replacement organ that pumps our physical blood around, but an inner newness of orientation that defies description in human words.

This hope extends beyond our lives in the present, or even in the decades or years that may still separate us from death. For of one thing we can be absolutely certain: death will one day – sooner or later – overtake us. It may creep slowly upon us in old age or may catch us much earlier by complete surprise, but it will come. And then? Is there hope beyond death? Well, maybe not in the way many people believe. Reincarnation has become a very popular belief, and not just among Hindus. It is the belief that life is lived in an ever continuing cycle. We have lived in some form before we were born, possibly as an animal or as another human being. We may even be able to discover aspects of our former lives. And we will continue to be reborn in one way or another. There is no basis for this kind of hope – and one might question whether this belief can be called 'hope' at all – either in the Bible or in experience.

The Christian hope is firmly based on the solid belief in a life in the hereafter. There may be some 'progressive' or 'liberal' theologians who prefer to remain neutral on the question of whether there is something after death. No one should deny these theologians the right to voice their opinions; but they should not confuse the issue by calling their opinion 'Christian'. Without the unfaltering conviction that Christ has conquered death and has brought real quality life within the reach of all who want to accept it, the Christian message is diluted to a humanistic philosophy. Read these words from the Bible. They are of such paramount importance that I quote them at some length:

'Now if Christ is preached as raised from the dead, how can some of you say that there is no resurrection of the dead? But if there is no resurrection of the dead, then Christ has not been raised; if Christ has not been raised, then our preaching is in vain and your faith is in vain. We are even found to be misrepresenting God, because we testified of God that he raised Christ, whom he did not raise if it is true that the dead are not raised. For if the dead are not raised, then Christ has not been raised. If Christ has not been raised, your faith is futile and you are still in your sins. Then those also who have fallen asleep in Christ have perished. If for this life only we have hoped in Christ, we are of all men most to be pitied.[56]

How should we view this continuation of our existence after death? Among Christians who believe in life after death, there has been a widespread and deep rooted idea that there is an invisible, immaterial something called 'soul' that is implanted in our body and is released the very moment we breathe our last breath. This sharp division between body and soul has of late lost much of its support among Christians, as many have begun to realize that it was based on Greek philosophy rather than on biblical teaching. A student of the history of the church will soon discover that many medieval and later scholars depended rather too heavily in much of their explanation of the Christian faith on the ideas of men like Plato and Aristotle. The Platonic philosophy of an eternal soul which is temporarily incarcerated in a mortal body, from which it is released at death, became very influential and many Christian believers neglected the question whether this idea was in fact supported by the Bible.

The biblical view of human nature is holistic: We are more than the chemical elements that compose our physical bodies. Our ability to respond to the divine, our affections, our will, and our religious experiences cannot be reduced to neurological or biological processes, however much these may be involved. Our identity is more than our DNA, even though we realize that our DNA is unique and makes each of us different from everybody else. What then happens when a person dies? If there is not an immortal something in you that is released at the moment of death, how would your death be different from that of your cat or dog?

The mystery of death and beyond

Death remains a mystery. No one can tell us what she experiences at the very end of her earthly existence. Of course, there are people with 'near-death' experiences who report that they have been in a long tunnel, with a dazzling light at the end, and have met a Figure in radiant garments whom they identified as an angel or as Jesus Christ. Some report that they saw how they were separated from their bodies and how the doctors bent over their body in a frantic (and successful) effort to save their life. But a *near*-death experience is just that. The people who experienced it have not actually died, and *near*-death phenomena cannot be taken as valid proof of what actually happens at the moment of real death.

It is significant that the Bible offers no clear-cut analysis of death. The word 'sleep' is repeatedly used to describe this intermediary stage between the life here and now and the life hereafter.[57] Obviously the word is not used in its everyday meaning, but it is apparently the best word available to us to indicate that death is (a) a period in which we are not conscious, and (b) a state from which we can return to consciousness. At the moment of death all consciousness of time is lost and in our perception the moment of death therefore coincides with our coming back to life. That is the only thing we need to know. Any further speculation about the 'nature of death' is futile. We can, however, be sure of a return to consciousness at the 'resurrection', and this forms a vital element of the hope of the Christian. This is, in particular, the point where those who have faith differ from those who don't. 'We do not want you to be ignorant', a Bible author writes, 'about those who fall asleep, or to grieve like the rest of men, who have no hope'.[58] Note how this statement refers to death as a state of 'sleep'. Note also, that death is cause for grief. That is true, regardless of whether one is a Christian or not. But the grief of the believer is of a different nature and is not like the mourning of those who have no hope. Whatever death is, it is only temporary. There is life beyond this short, and often miserable, existence on earth.

But, how can that be? As a child I heard about the 'resurrection' from death. I had been to the large cemetery in Amsterdam where my paternal grandparents had been buried. In my childish imagination I saw the heavy slab of granite slowly lifted on one side to make enough of an opening from which my grandfather and grandmother would climb from their grave. It did not take me long, however, before I began to realize that few human corpses survive the centuries reasonably intact, but that most bodies disintegrate within years. And then I realized that some bodies are incinerated and reduced to ashes, while some are eaten by ferocious animals. This realization challenged my belief in what I had been told by my parents. It bothered me to think that my little brother, who had died aged 8, would be resurrected as a child, while I supposed that my grandfather would return to life as an octogenarian. Later on, I learned that the cells of our bodies constantly die and are continually being replaced by new cells. I am still the same person as I was forty years ago, but all the material substance that formed my body four decades ago has died and disappeared. So, in a fashion, I have already survived death!

It is clear that our 'resurrection' does not depend on the safe keeping of the present material substances of our bodies. It depends on the power of our Designer-God to safeguard our identity and to recreate us at a given moment with a new (perfect) body that will never need any cosmetic surgery. I have no idea how he is going to do that. But there is nothing inherently more problematic in the re-creation of those people whose identity is safeguarded in the divine memory than in the processes that went into giving life to all things now living. Our hope is not based on anything we can verify with our intellect or our senses, but is fully justified once we have made the leap of faith and dared to accept the biblical information as a source of truth.

When we are raised from death to eternal life, there will be both continuity and discontinuity. We will have our past returned to us, but with fundamental changes and irreversible improvements. Somehow God stores in his heavenly computer all the data which make each person the unique being she is. The resurrected person does not consist of the same molecules or cells which made up her body during her life before death. This is not a necessary precondition to guarantee that the person is the same unique being, before as well as after death. When we step into a river on two consecutive days, we do not touch the same water, but we do step into the same river. An institution may move from one physical location to another and may get a completely different staff, and yet it can remain, in a very real sense, the same institution. Our resurrection from death is somewhat like that. Our new 'glorified' body will be very different from our present body, but we will nonetheless remain the very same unique being, with our memories, recognizable identity and personality. I love the way in which Adventist theologian Jack Provonsha expressed this encouraging aspect of the good news:

'The message of the Bible is that I *do* exist. Even in death I exist in the mind of God. . . . He provides the continuity between the now and the then. He who numbers the hairs of your head (in Jesus' metaphor) preserves (in our metaphor) the record of all that complex psycho-neurologic chemistry, the DNA and all that is associated, the memory, the personality, the character, and the behavourial peculiarities – each of which helps to constitute every precious individual person. He remembers and recreates it all at the appointed time, at the resurrection.'[59]

We should not ask scientific questions such as where all molecules of our present bodies remain. What matters is my identity, and the lasting significance of my life and destiny! 'God loves more than just the molecules which happen to be part of my body at the moment of my death,' says Wilhelm Breuning, a systematic theologian.

'He loves a body which shows the signs of the burdens it has carried, and of the restless longing of its pilgrimage, which have left during this pilgrimage many traces in a world, which by these traces has become more human. . . . The resurrection of the body means that God, because of his love, does not allow anything to be lost. He has collected all dreams, and no smile escaped his attention. The resurrection of the body means that man does not only rediscover his last moment, but all of his history.'[60]

Somehow, Jesus' victory over death has made *our* victory over death possible. 'God raised the Lord and will also raise us up by his power'.[61] There is no way we can understand all the implications of this astonishing fact. But the apostle John points our thinking in the right direction. 'Beloved', he says, 'we are God's children now; it does not yet appear what we shall be, but we know that when he appears we shall be like [Christ], for we shall see him as he is.'[62]

The Christ who was raised from the dead was the same person as the One who a few days earlier died on the cross. He arose with a 'glorified' body which was no longer subject to the laws of nature in the way our present mortal bodies are, but which, nevertheless, possessed a continuity with the 'human form' he had prior to his death and resurrection.[63] He was the same Person, recognizable by his outward appearance, his voice and his gestures. That gives us good reason to conclude that in our new 'glorious bodies' we will be recognized by those we knew in this life and will enjoy the life beyond with us.

Hope for the world

In painting the hope of the believer the Bible does not stop at the hope for the individual. There is also hope for the world. In a dual sense: hope even now in the midst of global hopelessness, and hope for another world which is yet to come. Faith in a God who has everything under control, in spite of all the appearances to the contrary, allows us to have hope even in this world. Faith enables us to see more than the chaos in war-torn countries in Africa and the violence in the Middle East. It makes us see more than ethnic hatred, religious bigotry and global greed, and more than poverty and hunger. And, nearer home, it allows us to see more than amusement-seeking consumerism, greedy materialism, shallow egotism and hypocrisy. It also makes us aware of the beauty and goodness that is still boundlessly manifest in this world, in the servant leadership of many great men and women, and in the love and kindness that motivates many people in all corners of the earth. Faith will always alert us to the positive things that can happen even in the midst of suffering and tragedy; to the inspiring examples of self-denial and humility in the midst of violence and corruption. Faith never sees a world totally beyond hope.

But faith is also realistic. When we read the Bible and try to discover what the future will be like, we find that it frequently refers to the end of this world and to a new beginning. In spite of the many wonderful things the eye of faith sees, and the hope it gives regarding this world, it also alerts us to the fact that, in the long term, this present world is beyond salvage. Postmodernism has cruelly, but justifiably, exploded the myth of continuous progress. The First World War, the Russian Revolution, the Great Depression of the thirties, the Second World War, the 'cold war', Korea and Vietnam, the conflicts in the Gulf and in the former Yugoslavia, the war in Iraq, the never-ending problems of the developing world, the repeated energy crises, and a slowly but surely dying environment, have largely destroyed the optimism of former generations. There is a constant fear in the back of our minds that mankind may destroy itself and that too little has been done too late to solve the gigantic problems of mankind.

Jacques Piccard, the son of Auguste Piccard (the famous co-worker of Einstein) and himself a prominent scientist, once said in an interview, 'I see in the future nothing but the suicide of mankind.'[64] Jean-Paul Sartre advised us to have a good look at ourselves and to ask ourselves whether we can tolerate what we see. Looking carefully at ourselves, he said, we see an ever further progressing dehumanization, a 'striptease' of our humanity.[65]

Fortunately, our hope reaches beyond the world as it is. We have already quoted these words: 'If only for this life we have hope in Christ, we are to be pitied more than all men.'[66] Long before Christ entered this world his coming had been predicted. True to those promises, he did indeed come. Manifold are the promises also that he will come for a second time. He said so himself: 'I will come back!'[67] On the final page of the Bible this promise is repeated: 'Yes, I am coming soon.'[68] This is the hope that binds the Christian believers together. It is – and I am quoting the Bible again – 'the blessed hope: the glorious appearing of our great God and Saviour, Jesus Christ.'[69] When he comes, this world meets its grand finale. Words are inadequate to capture the good news: 'The first heaven and the first earth' will 'pass away' and will be replaced by 'a new heaven and a new earth.'[70]

If your curiosity has been awakened, get your Bible and read about what God has in store for us. And find some good books that help you further understand the meaning of what you read. But even then many things will remain a mystery – at least for the time being. What will we be like? And what will the 'new' world be like? Though John, one of Christ's initial group of disciples, tells us that, on the one hand, we will be 'like Christ', he adds in the same passage that it 'does not yet appear what we shall be.'[71]

In particular in the final chapters of the Bible we find information about the 'new world'. Much of it is in highly symbolic language. It is, in fact, easier to understand which things will *no longer* be part of our future experience than to comprehend the things which will be. God 'will wipe away every tear from [our] eyes, and death shall be no more, neither shall there be mourning or crying nor pain any more'.[72] Through the ages these words have never ceased to give comfort; and they encourage us today. No more death! No more slowly deteriorating bodies, no heart attacks, no polio, no malaria, no AIDS, no cancer – not even a bout of flu! No more sadness, no more goodbyes, and no more disillusionment!

And there is more good news. 'But as for the cowardly, the faithless, the polluted, as for murderers, fornicators, sorcerers, idolaters, and all liars,' they are noticeably absent.[73] Just try to imagine what that means: No more dishonesty, no more people you cannot trust, no more incest or deceit, no more addictions, no more occult rituals, and no more people who see nothing but themselves. All things that frighten us in today's world have miraculously disappeared. No more instruments of war: no nuclear bombs, or weapons of mass destruction; no hole in the ozone layer; no pollution of the environment; no desertification and no tsunamis; no Taliban or Al Qaida; no need for political asylum; no hunger; no homelessness. Everything that could threaten our happiness in any way has been for ever removed. The future of mankind is safe and secure. That is all included in the Christian hope.

Is it too good to be true? It would be, if there is no God who once made us and continues to care for us. Admittedly, there is no definite proof other than the deep inner assurance that results from our leap of faith! But these beliefs make glorious sense, and are truly 'justifiable' once we accept the reality of God and are willing to listen to what he has communicated.

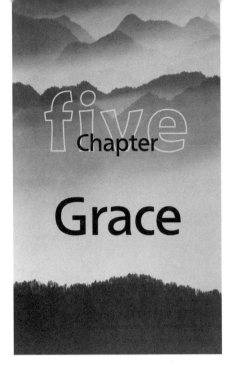

Chapter five

Grace

Let me begin this chapter by reminding you of what I said in the introduction. The existence of 'evil' has always been a problem which has turned many people away from the Christian faith. For how in the world can a loving God, who is said to be all-powerful, allow the terrible things we see around us? This is a particularly thorny issue for postmodern people who have learned to distrust any of those 'grand narratives' that are seen as attempting to explain the reality of evil away. But, difficult though it may be, we must deal with it.

In this chapter we are confronted with two aspects of the Christian faith that are best described as 'mysteries'. For we shall see that whatever we say about these mysteries, as we grapple with all kinds of questions surrounding them, it will not provide a clear-cut, totally satisfactory answer to all aspects. But in spite of the fact that we will be left with many unanswered and unanswerable questions, we will also, during this phase of our exploratory journey, make some magnificent discoveries which will, once again, fit into our ever strengthening web of 'justifiable' beliefs. I believe these ongoing discoveries will most definitely show a cohesive accord with the conclusions in the earlier chapters. I am asking you to look with as open a mind as you can possibly bring to it, on the one hand at the 'mystery of sin' and evil, and, on the other hand, at the 'mystery of divine grace'.

The mystery of evil

'Sin' (or one of its many synonyms) is a keyword in most religions. We have used it already a few times without attempting to define the term. We will do so in this chapter. To go against the will of the gods, or of Allah, or of the Christian God, is called 'sin'. To do what has been expressly forbidden by the deity is sin. For most postmodern people, however, the term has become quite meaningless. We may, they say, in all honesty have to recognize that we possess some defects in our character, and we may have to work diligently on some aspects of our personality and to improve the ways in which we relate to problems or to other people, but it is basically within our own reach to remedy these imperfections. People may suffer the unfortunate consequences from having grown up in lamentable circumstances and may have undergone negative influences, but that does not mean that they must be classified as 'bad' or 'sinful' people.

Well, however sympathetic it may sound, this argumentation does not hold water. The stark reality of everyday life tells a different story. It is an undeniable fact that, although we see a lot of goodness and honesty in people around us, we cannot fail also to notice plenty of egoism, greed, ruthlessness and corruption. The wrongs we see are, unfortunately, more than superficial defects which people can outgrow in due time. And we have to admit that there are also people, all around the world, one has to describe as totally *evil*. It is not difficult to name some examples. Almost automatically the name of the German Führer, Adolf Hitler, comes to mind, the evil brain behind the Holocaust – probably the greatest of crimes ever committed. And that of Pol Pot, the evil genius behind the Khmer Rouge and the killing fields of Cambodia in the 1970s. But there are many more evil men (and some women) who tortured and killed to satisfy their thirst for power and to ensure that any competition for their position would be eliminated before it would pose any real threat.

Just think of men like Uganda's Idi-Amin, who ruled that country with a bloody fist from 1971 to 1979, and of the self-styled emperor Jean Bedel Bokassa in the Central African Republic (1966-1979), who was known to drink the blood of his enemies and to enjoy eating human flesh. Think also of two more recent examples of personified evil: Iraq's Saddam Hussein, and the instigator of 9/11: Osama bin Laden.

There are many additional examples of evil people, who made the headlines for a few weeks and then disappeared again from public view as the news would begin to focus on other brutalities. The older generation remembers Charles Manson and his destructive doomsday cult which was responsible for at least eight grisly murders in the 1960s. I well remember the reports about serial killer Jeffrey Dahmer (1960-1994) in Chicago, as I was living in the United States at the time when he was daily in the news. He killed at least seventeen men and admitted to eating parts of them. One thinks also of the person who was often described as the most hated woman in England, Myra Hindly, who, together with her lover, murdered three children. And the list could go on.

Yes, the wicked deeds of some people cannot adequately be described in terms of mere 'shortcomings', 'lack of judgement', or 'character defects'; even the word 'evil' seems too positive to define their terrible acts.

In addition to personal 'sin' and evil in individuals, there is also a dimension to many of the wrongs of this world which cannot be pinned on a few individuals but is of a corporate nature (even though it remains, of course, the end result of what countless individuals have set in motion and either intentionally or subconsciously promote and support). The inequality in the world between the rich and the poor, the endemic injustice in many societies, the widespread corruption in certain developing countries as well as in large western business corporations, the rigging of elections and the wilful destruction of the environment – they are all patent examples of corporate evil.

Corporate evil can assume an even uglier face in the relentless looting and merciless raping of women and children by soldiers (on all sides) in civil and regional wars. Corporate evil manifested itself in the gruelling trenches on the battle fields of the Great War of 1914-1918, which many have forgotten but which was one of the greatest and most brutal tragedies of human history; in the deadly blasts of the nuclear devices over the skies of Hiroshima and Nagasaki, and the relentless bombardments of German cities by the allied forces in World War II and of cities like London and Rotterdam by the Luftwaffe; and in such far away places as Korea and Vietnam, Sudan and Iraq.

Is it a wonder that people turn away from belief in God? How can we believe, they say, in a God of goodness and love, who 'sits on his throne in his high heaven' but fails to use his supposedly unlimited powers to prevent all this personal and corporate evil, or at least to step in and call it to a halt? And that is not even considering all these other things which cause people to wonder where this loving God is when tragedy strikes – when a wife and mother dies of breast cancer at age 45; when a child gets killed by a drunk driver; when thousands drown in floods in Bangladesh; when so many people see everything they possess swept away during a hurricane? And this list goes on almost *ad infinitum*.

These questions are not new. Through the ages people have asked: Why? In our time, however, this type of question is asked with ever increasing intensity. The traditional answers are not good enough for postmodern people. Life is so blatantly unfair to so many. How does that fit with a God who is supposed to be just and perfect, and who is promoted by Christians as a God of love?

I cannot pretend that I have a complete answer that will immediately and totally suppress the cries of protest and incomprehension, and will instantaneously remove the deep-felt mistrust towards such a God. For in final analysis there cannot be a satisfactory explanation in human terms for the existence of sin and evil. There is no explanation for the fact that things could go so utterly wrong in a universe that resulted from a perfect design. Has a perfect God (that is what he must be if we can call him 'God') allowed for a fundamental flaw in his design? Did someone or something throw a spanner in the works? The Bible refers to a Satan and to 'evil angels', who fell from their original state of perfection. But how come? How could that happen? There is no good answer to these burning questions. The origin of evil remains a mystery.[74]

But however mystifying the origin of evil may be, its reality is undeniable and universal. There is not a single human being who is unaffected by it. 'There is no one righteous, not even one', declares the apostle Paul as he writes to the church in Rome, quoting from a psalm.[75] 'All have sinned and fall short of the glory of God.'[76] Every human being is to some extent co-responsible for the existence of evil in his own life and in the world. But there is more to it than that. Whenever humans do something wrong, there is a power in the background, who encouraged this act of wrong-doing. This power is referred to as a 'killer' from the very beginning, who started cosmic warfare against God, as we saw in the previous chapter. Therefore, in a way, evil is both *super*human and *sub*human. It is subhuman because it destroys the full human potential that God designed for his creatures. And it is superhuman in that man has become a participant in that cosmic combat which involves sinister powers which human beings cannot fight in their own limited, natural strength.[77] Truly, all of this in many ways remains a 'mystery', but that does not make it less of an awful reality.

The even greater mystery

The 'mystery of evil' is, however, more than offset by another mystery: the 'mystery of grace'. It belongs to the core of the Christian 'good news' that somehow God has taken care of the evil in the universe and that he did so through the death of Jesus Christ. A major part of this chapter will deal with that event and its implications. I will not deny that it takes another, quite considerable, leap of faith to accept that a single event which took place in the Middle East almost two thousand years ago has provided the definitive solution to the problem of evil, meaningless suffering, death and decay. But it all fits together and makes glorious sense once you have dared to step out in faith. Once again, it does not mean that we will find a rational explanation for every aspect of what God did for us through his 'Son' Jesus Christ. Yet, the 'mystery of iniquity' is met head on by the 'mystery of godliness'.[78] Charles Scriven, in his 'theological ABC', which is still very much worth reading, puts it very succinctly in these words:

'Here is the great mystery, of course. Just why this particular death was crucial or just how it worked is something not even the New Testament writers undertake to explain.

'The *how* of the cross, for them as for us, is a puzzle. But the *what* of the cross – the fact that one death has put the world into a new relationship with the divine – is a matter of certainty.'[79]

And he adds:

'The story of how God defeated the enemy is surely the most splendid paradox you will ever come across. For he did not horsewhip anyone, begin guerrilla warfare, or issue intimidating threats. Instead, he defeated the enemy by an act of powerlessness, by dying at the cross. The testimony of the first believers is that Jesus, the Son of God, "freed us from our sins by his blood"' (Revelation 1:5).[80]

But we are getting ahead of the story and first need to discuss two important concepts in order to lay the ground for our further explorations into the mysterious Truth (for that is what it is) of the atonement (or at-*one*-ment) which God provided when he bridged the abyss that the 'mystery of evil' had created between him and us.

Sin and guilt: what are we talking about?

Before we go any further, the concept of *sin* will need to be defined more precisely. What is the biblical meaning of this word that is so widely, and often so flippantly, used? Is there a definitive norm which tells us whether or not an action is a sin? Or is this a totally subjective matter, depending on custom and tradition rather than on any objective standard? At this point the spirit of postmodernism and the voice of the Bible critically differ. Postmodern people have a problem with absolute truth and absolute moral norms. And many Christians would concur with part of their criticism: quite a few things have in the past been called 'sin' by priests and pastors without any real basis in the writings of Scripture, and talk about 'sin' has too often been used, or rather abused, to control and manipulate people.

But if we accept that there is a God who made us and is interested in us, it stands to reason that we should order our relationship with him in ways that he approves of and which will lead to greater happiness. Seen from that perspective we understand the statement made by the prophet Isaiah when he wanted to redirect the thinking of the people he was called to minister to: 'Your iniquities [a synonym for 'sins'] have separated you from your God; your sins have hidden his face from you.'[81] Sin is, in essence, everything that separates human beings from God. Or, to quote another biblical passage: 'Everything that does not come from faith is sin.'[82]

That is a good point of departure. But how do we translate this into something more concrete? What are some of these things which drive a barrier between us and our Maker? Asked for specifics, the average person in the Middle Ages would be able to list seven 'deadly' sins which were seen as the key vices that caused estrangement between man and God: pride, envy, gluttony, lust, anger, greed, and sloth. This list may be worth considering even today. But making lists tends to have a major disadvantage. As soon as you do so, you will inevitably also forget certain things, and there will always be people who will say: It's OK, for it's not on the list!' Rather than to catalogue specific actions and label some of these as 'sin', we would do much better to look at underlying principles, while we keep in mind that the Bible does not only condemn sinful outward actions but also focuses on inward motives. That makes perfect sense. For outward actions may give a totally warped picture of what really makes people tick, and if we could discern people's true motives, we would in many cases look at them with fresh eyes. The trouble, of course, is that we can usually only guess at the motives of others. At times we may not even be clear about our own real motivations. Only God is able to see beyond the external deed and 'knows the hearts of all men.'[83]

Do we at least have some broad, guiding principles? Yes, we do. They are usually referred to as the Ten Commandments. They date in their present form from the middle of the second millennium BC, when, after the escape of the Hebrew people from their Egyptian bondage, the nation of Israel was founded and God provided them with a constitution.[84] The first four of these ten principles deal with the relationship of man towards his God, while principles five to ten provide basic guidelines for the ways in which we relate to fellow human beings.

The first four of these guidelines tell us not to mix our worship of God with the veneration of other gods (idols) and not to worship human artefacts as representations of the divine. They tell us not to use God's name in inappropriate ways and to dedicate a weekly segment of our time – each seventh day – in a special way to God. We will return to this particular point, for this fourth principle is of enormous significance. The next six principles tell us about the sanctity of the family, of marriage, of physical life, and of property, and emphasize the danger of playing with the truth, while the tenth principle focuses on the insidious evil of envy. These guidelines have lost nothing of their actuality and have, in fact, inspired the compilers of most civil codes.

Going against the principles of the Ten Commandment law is sin. 'Sin is lawlessness', we are told.[85] But there is also another dimension to sin. It is not just a matter of doing wrong things, or of neglecting these principles and refusing to apply them to everyday life, or of having the wrong motives. It is not just a matter of hatred and murder, of deceit, of envy or immorality. Sin is also failing to achieve what we might have accomplished if we had really tried. It is also a failure to live up to our potential and to fall short of the ideal. One of the Hebrew words found in the original manuscripts of the Bible which is translated as 'sin' has the root meaning of 'missing the mark.' Surely, there is no one who can boast to be sinless when the full biblical sense of the word 'sin' is taken into account.

In addition, there is another aspect to be mentioned. Even though many people have only the vaguest notion of what sin really is, they may, however paradoxical that appears to be, suffer from serious guilt. One might say that the experience of guilt is positive: it proves that our conscience – our inner compass as to what is right and wrong, which apparently is part of the basic fabric of human beings – still functions properly, or at least still 'works' in some rudimentary way. Some only occasionally experience a faint twinge of guilt when they realize they have done something they should not have. Countless others, however, suffer from intense guilt because of things that have gone wrong, unwise decisions they have made, and one-time chances they have missed. They realize that they have made other people suffer and wish they could undo their mistakes and pull back the words which should not have escaped from their mouth. They feel a tremendous guilt because they cheated on their partner, they neglected their children, or ruined their health through addictive habits. They look back with a deep sense of remorse at the years they have wasted and at the solemn promises they have broken.

Many of those who suffer from guilt 'complexes' may need counselling from a psychologist or a pastor. They must be delivered from the past and from its dark secrets, and must have professional help to find a new lease on life, without constantly returning in their minds to the things that cause them so much regret, and without being immobilised by any trauma caused by their past mistakes. But the true and complete remedy for guilt goes far beyond the benefits of psychological or even pastoral counselling. Because the removal of guilt is not primarily a matter of what humans can do themselves. The solution must come from 'above'.

Finally, we should be clear that sin leads nowhere. Or, more precisely, it leads to death, to nothingness. Not just to the temporary kind of death that comes to all of us and may be compared to the kind of 'sleep' referred to earlier. It is possible to 'awake' from that kind of death. We can have life beyond this temporary death if we accept the offer of life that is available. But if our sins are not somehow cancelled out, they will lead to a state of permanent death, one of never-ending nothingness. The biblical term for this is 'the second death'[86], popularly referred to as 'hell'.

Dealing with the problem of sin and evil

A few points stand out as we consider the scope of the sin-problem. Sin and guilt, as we saw, are larger than we are. The solution is not found in a rational acknowledgment that some things are wrong and that we, unfortunately, fail to meet an objective standard of conduct. No, many will continue to feel depressed and miserable and will experience a life-long sense of guilt which they cannot shake off by any kind of rationalisation and good intentions for the future.

Let us now, however, take things a step further and try to look at the issue from God's perspective. Of course (and this cannot be repeated often enough), we cannot expect to see the full picture, but we can catch some glimpses, to the extent that God has communicated some aspects of his views and dealings with us. To put it in very simplistic words, which admittedly fail to do justice to this lofty topic: God decided to deal with the sin-problem in a radical and decisive manner. Or, to state it more correctly: *He has, in actual fact, already dealt with the problem!* In spite of what we may think as we look around us in this world: The arch-enemy of human fulfilment and joy has already been defeated!

Humanly speaking, it would seem that God had a number of options in dealing with the issue of sin.

1. God could have designed us in a way that would have been fault proof. But beings which have no will of their own and cannot make their own decisions are no more than mechanical robots. Had God opted for this approach, concepts such as goodness and service would have been utterly meaningless.

2. God could have intervened after the first occurrence of sin and could have eliminated the sinners. He could have started all over again, with a clean slate. It is not difficult to see how the objections which apply to No. 1 also apply here.

3. God could also have abandoned his creation as soon as he saw that things had gone sour. If he had done so, human history would soon have ended, for sin, if not tempered by any power of good, is by definition totally self-destructive.

4. God wants to be loved by his creatures, and love cannot be forced. It presupposes the exercise of a free will. Giving his creatures a free will was a risk, but one that could not be avoided, if there was to be a meaningful service of true love. When God's creatures used their free will by choosing to rebel, God came with a 'plan'. He would remove the sins of this world, by stepping into the arena of sin and evil himself – by conquering sin in a way that would leave no doubt whatsoever about what he stands for, and in a way that would eventually guarantee the total eradication of everything that has the faintest taint of sin. It would be a costly solution, but the only one which would do justice to human free will as well as to divine love.

One might argue that this is very human language, and also that God might still have had other options. That might well be, but we are approaching a realm where the human mind cannot enter. Once again there will be more questions than human beings can find answers to. One thing is, however, absolutely certain: God could not ignore the problem. A holy God cannot tolerate what goes against his very nature. Sin makes him angry. Not in the way we might become angry, as our anger is often irrational, selective, or even capricious. God abhors sin, it goes against everything he wants and is. So he chose option four, because of who and what he is. That is what a key text in the Bible affirms:

'For God so loved the world that he gave his one and only Son, that whoever believes in him shall not perish, but have everlasting life.'[87] Or, as it is stated elsewhere: 'He loved us, and sent his Son as an atoning sacrifice for our sins.'[88]

So, what do these words mean? What happened? Jesus Christ suffered and died. There is no doubt that we are dealing with a historical event. On a Friday afternoon, around the year AD31, on a hill on the outskirts of Jerusalem, a man known as Jesus of Nazareth was executed by Roman soldiers. The victim of a fanatical conspiracy of the national clergy, he was arrested, received a mock trial and was condemned to death by crucifixion. It was a form of execution which was invented by the Carthaginians, but adopted and 'refined' by the Romans. Before being nailed to a wooden pole, which the condemned person himself had to carry to the place of execution, the victim was scourged with a whip made of leather straps to which sharp pieces of bone were attached. Suspended in the heat of the day between heaven and earth, he would suffer from terrible dehydration and excruciating pain as the weight of the body would tear at the wounds in hands and feet. The suffering, which could continue for as long as a full day or more, was cut short in Jesus' case because of the religious scruples of the clergy who had engineered the entire affair. With their distorted sense of values they wanted the unpleasant affair over and done with before sunset, so that they would not desecrate their holy day! Read the entire story in the gospel[89] and do not stop at the point where Jesus cried out: 'It is finished!' Continue, and also read about what happened some thirty-six hours later when the tomb in which Jesus' body had been laid, was found miraculously empty. Not because the body had been stolen, as Jesus' enemies tried to make people believe, but because he had risen from the grave and was alive! *Death had not been able to contain him*.

Terrible though this ignominious death was, some people have suffered even greater pain and died even more torturous deaths. What makes this Jesus story unique? Why is it that Christians have ever since called Jesus Christ their 'Saviour'? Theologians have sorted through all the biblical evidence and come up with a variety of theories. Technically, these can be divided into theories which propose an *objective* atonement and those that argue for a *subjective* atonement. The difference is more than a matter of words but is, in fact, crucial. Those who plead for the idea of an objective atonement say that the sin problem has been dealt with there and then in what happened in Jerusalem. Something took place on that Friday afternoon in Jerusalem that changed the entire picture of God-man relationships and provided atonement. What happened at the cross and in the tomb resulted in 'salvation' for all people who are eager to have it. Through this event their status before God changed decisively.

But the proponents of subjective theories of atonement come at the topic from a totally different angle. Salvation is not so much the result of an objective event outside of us, they say, but it rather takes place *in* us. We become changed and freed from our sinful inclinations as we contemplate the incomparable love and self-giving that was manifested in the life and, in particular, in those final moments of the earthly life of Christ, our supreme role model.

I do not believe that we have to choose between the objective and the subjective view. Both points of view are, I am convinced, valid and complement each other. I am thankful for the insights I have gained from reading numerous theological books on this subject, but I have concluded long ago that the 'mystery of love', which resulted in the death of Jesus Christ on the cross, cannot be captured adequately in any neat theory. Richard Rice fully concurs:

'What did Jesus' death accomplish? How does it solve the problem of sin? The New Testament gives no single answer to this question. There is no one theory of atonement in the apostolic writings; in fact, there are no theories at all. What we find instead are several striking metaphors, or symbols, describing what Jesus did.'[90]

The Himalaya of God's grace

What are some of these metaphors or symbols and what do they tell us? The kind of theory one arrives at depends on which metaphors one emphasizes. In describing what Jesus' death meant the Bible writers often used language that was reminiscent of the sacrificial services that went on in the Old Testament sanctuary of the people of Israel. When John the Baptist introduced his slightly younger cousin Jesus to the crowds, strikingly enough he referred to him as 'the *Lamb* of God, who takes away the sins of the world'.[91] We get a better idea of what this means if we know something of what happened in the sanctuary services of ancient Israel – first in a movable tent and later in a magnificent permanent temple complex in Jerusalem. The rituals, which are described in great detail in the book of Leviticus, with their daily and annual sacrifices, were not simply a system that Israel had borrowed from their neighbors in the Middle East. It was a constant and vivid reminder to the entire nation that something 'from the outside' was needed to restore the relationship between God and his creatures. Everything that happened in these services was a masterful *tableau vivant*, a dramatic illustration of how God would eventually deal with sin. The blood of the animals that was shed had no merit in itself, but it represented the blood of the One who would come into this world from above, would live a perfect life and would eventually be sacrificed. It was God's intention that the people of ancient Israel would begin to understand that sin was an extremely costly business requiring an expensive solution. It was a matter of life and death.

The writers of the parts of the Bible that were written after Jesus had lived and died on this earth understood the connection. Jesus, the apostle John said, 'is the atoning sacrifice for our sins, and not only for ours, but also for the sins of the whole world.'[92] This is what Christians are referring to when, echoing a text from the Bible, they sing about having been saved 'by the precious blood of the Lamb.'[93]

Another set of metaphors suggests a kind of judicial arrangement. There was a debt (caused by the accumulated sin of mankind) that had to be paid. The life of Jesus was the supreme payment that was necessary to buy us free from the 'bondage' of evil. Here we also find a motive which was derived from the Israel's past. When God gave his laws to the descendents of Abraham, as they were about to occupy the land that God had destined for them, they received a package of regulations and statutes. The Ten Commandments were the core, but there was also a vast array of laws that regulated weekly, monthly and annual holy days, the rituals in the sanctuary and the lives of those who officiated in these rituals. Other laws dealt with matters that we would today regard as 'civil', still others dealt with issues of health and even diet. Among this legal package was an arrangement which was meant to prevent the accumulation of riches in the hands of a few. If someone had been forced to sell a property in order to survive, there was a possibility that, under certain conditions, this property could be 'redeemed' (bought back). A 'ransom' could be paid by a kinsman so that the property would return to the original owner. This language was adopted by the early Christians as they struggled to find adequate words for the 'mystery of grace'. We have, they said, 'redemption in his blood.'[94] 'We are bought with a price', it is stated elsewhere.[95] That was in full accordance with what Christ himself had said. He had come to 'give his life as a ransom for many.'[96]

One Bible writer in particular, the apostle Paul, theorized more than others about the meaning of Christ's death. He often used legal terminology which has played a significant role in the history of Christianity, in the age of the famous fourth-century scholar and church leader Augustine, but especially since the split between Roman Catholicism and Protestantism in the early sixteenth century. He talked about justification by faith, i.e. that we are declared 'just' (perfect, sinless), not because we have succeeded in shaking off the shackles of sin ourselves, having found a clever self-help method to improve our characters to the point that God no longer thinks of us as sinful, *but because Jesus took our place*. We should have suffered the consequences of sin: eternal death and nothingness. Had that become our fate we would not have had grounds for any valid complaints. But what actually happened was that Jesus Christ stepped in. He was our 'substitute', we might say. Paul's argument in his letter to the Romans may not be easy to follow for novices in Bible reading, but give it a try even if you feel you are in that class. You may have to skip some details you find as yet hard to understand, but you will get the general idea: Christ died in our place. We (i.e. all human beings together) have fallen miserably short of the divine ideal; we have rebelled against it, and therefore deserve to be punished. That punishment would be eternal death, for that is the inevitable, ultimate result of estrangement from God, the Source of life. But here God takes the initiative. Jesus Christ comes to this world, and takes over the punishment that would have been ours, had he not intervened.[97]

When theologians seek to explain what all of this means, they use words like 'satisfaction' and 'substitution', and one can easily get the impression that all of this is a matter of cold forensics. But let us not fall into the trap of reducing the 'mystery of grace' to a sort of debit and credit arrangement, where the load of our sins is carefully weighed against Christ's innocence! There is, indeed, an important element of substitution and of satisfaction, but there is much more involved than that. What Christ did was not something an angry God demanded in order that his sense of justice would be satisfied, but it was something a loving God provided.

In one of the most beautiful chapters of the Bible, we find a moving poem about 'the suffering servant of God', which has always been understood as pointing beyond its eighth century BC imagery to the passion and death of the One, the Messiah, Israel had been eagerly awaiting for centuries. Although referred to as 'a man', this 'suffering servant' is led to the slaughter like a 'lamb', as 'he bore the sins of many.' Here indeed is a most touching portrait of the person Christians now refer to as their Saviour:

'He had no beauty or majesty to attract us to him, nothing in his appearance that we should desire him.

'He was despised and rejected by men, a man of sorrows, and familiar with suffering. . . .

'Surely he took up our infirmities and carried our sorrows, yet we considered him stricken by God, smitten by him and afflicted.

'But *he was pierced for our transgressions*, he was crushed for our iniquities; the punishment that brought us peace was upon him, and by his wounds we are healed.

'We all like sheep have gone astray, each of us has turned to his own way; and *the Lord laid upon him the iniquity of us all*.

'He was oppressed and afflicted, yet he did not open his mouth; *he was led like a lamb to the slaughter*, and as a sheep before her shearers is silent, so he did not open his mouth. . . .

'He was assigned a grave with the wicked, and with the rich in his death, though he had done no violence, nor was any deceit in his mouth. . . .

'He poured his life out unto death, and was numbered with the transgressors. For *he bore the sin of many*, and made intercession for the transgressors.'[98]

As we have already stated, the Bible itself does not provide a full-blown theory of the atonement, but is content with providing a number of striking word pictures which speak with greater clarity than a tome on theology would do. These metaphors complement each other; they stimulate us in a powerful way in our meditation, but they should not be taken in isolation from each other, and beyond their illustrative intentions. We fail to do justice to the 'mystery of grace' if we attempt to reduce everything to a rational formula. No abstracted theory can describe the entire truth – theories usually emphasize just one aspect. Too often theories place God's love over and against his justice, as if he changes moods and must be persuaded to be gracious. The Bible therefore uses many word pictures, all expressing something of the grand, but inexpressible good news that things between God and the beings he designed are once again OK. I fully agree with Adventist theologian Richard Rice:

'Perhaps we need a variety of views of Christ's work. A great natural wonder like the Grand Canyon of the Himalayas invites us to look at it from many vantage points. It never ceases to impress us. And no one perspective captures its grandeur. To a far greater degree, Christ's accomplishments defy our powers of description. The more we reflect upon the meaning of the cross, the more amazing it becomes. God's condescension in assuming humanity and his mysterious willingness to bear the consequences of sin will challenge our minds and stir our emotions forever. Eternity will not be time enough to plumb the depths of love revealed at Calvary.'[99]

There is, however, one additional point that needs to be underlined. This description of the 'mystery of grace' seems too easy. Something went terribly wrong: sin entered the world. And all of us have been affected. While we all come into this world with some considerable inherited chips on our shoulders and with lamentably negative traits that we can trace back to our ancestry, yet most of us will have no trouble in seeing that we have frequently done and said, of our own volition, things we knew were wrong. Our inner voice told us what to do, but we consciously chose to go against it, or we deliberately did not live up to what we knew we should have done. And so, although lots of questions remain, we cannot just turn around and say, the devil made me do it. Or, unfortunately, it is in the genes which I have inherited. No one can claim that he has no responsibility whatsoever for his sins.

And surely, if you are responsible for wrong things, you have to make amends. That is true if you have caused pain to your neighbour, or have stolen someone's bike or damaged public property. When you come to the point that you acknowledge what you have done, you will, of course, try to make amends to the people who were hurt or disadvantaged, whenever possible. And it is quite understandable that there are many who feel that they must also do *their* part in restoring the impaired relationship between them and God. It cannot be so simple, they say, that we can just hold out our hand and that God provides his 'salvation' for free, no strings attached – thank you. Well, maybe there are strings attached to most gifts, but what God gives does come free.

This goes against the grain of life. The reality of today's world is that nothing that has any real value is free. It is therefore little wonder that ever since sin entered the world, people have tried to grab the initiative, and have felt the need to do all they can to arrange for compensation and to appease their gods or God. In cultures around the world, people have developed extensive rituals to find favour with their gods, trying to make peace with them by sacrificing their possessions, even their children, in their desperate attempts to strike an acceptable bargain with heaven. If you study the various world religions carefully, you will find that usually the onus is placed on man to bridge the gap between earth and heaven. But here is where the Christian religion is unique. 'In the Christian view of things, efforts to find peace that begin by human initiative and human power do not produce peace at all but only greater and greater anguish. Such efforts do not take care of sin, because – and this is the key point – they are themselves sinful.'[100]

Nothing we do ourselves will make a scrap of difference in the solution of the sin-problem. Only a Source of true unending life is able to provide that kind of life to creatures who have lost it. Christ could not have accomplished what he did, had he not been who he was! The sinless One, who remained sinless while on earth in the midst of sin (and in the face of more temptations than we will ever have to face) is such a Source of eternal life.

This is what the concept of 'grace' is all about. It is free, 'gratis.' That is difficult to accept for many of us who live at the beginning of the twenty-first century. We want to earn and deserve the things we value and do not like to wait, together with everyone else, for free hand-outs. However, we will have to swallow our pride and humbly ask for God's free gift. He is not throwing it at us or forcing it down our throats. It is, in a very urgent sense, a matter of *take* it or leave it! But, if we do take it, something extraordinary happens. And here we are back at the subjective element of the miracle of salvation. The actual experience of countless people teaches us that accepting the free gift of grace changes human beings. It changes us in the way we think and behave, and in the way we set our priorities.

There has been an ongoing controversy in the Christian world between 'works' and 'faith.' It has to do with the question of what you need to do in order to find favour with God. Some say you must first show that you want to be good and prove to be obedient to divine instructions before you can be a recipient of God's salvation offer. Others say, No, God's gift comes free, there is nothing you can do to earn it by anything you do. And therefore, what your actions are is virtually of no importance! What this second groups says is true, except for the last clause. For those who have reached out for the free gift of grace and have received it and stored it in their hearts, will want to bring their lives in line with whatever God has indicated is best for them. One might therefore say: human 'works' do not lead to this healing of the breach between ourselves and God, but our 'works' will follow our acceptance of the free gift of grace as a natural expression of our gratefulness!

The cross was an unparalleled demonstration of God's infinite love and it cannot but elicit a human response of deep appreciation. It so impresses us that it gives us strength; it results in a determination to change our attitudes of egoism and self-centredness. Allowing ourselves to become immersed in this atmosphere of self-giving will influence us profoundly and will make us stand back in awe: *So much love!* It moves us, it transforms us. But having said that, we must come full circle. It is not our reaction that brings us back to God. The cross – and we cannot emphasize this too much and too often – is more than a heroic example of suffering which moves us and motivates us to become better people. There are other examples of great suffering and heroic death which may also inspire us. We are saved because 'the mystery of grace' is so much more than just an inspiring example. And it is, in fact, part of the 'mystery of grace' that, once we have opened ourselves to it, we discover a hitherto unknown inner strength to order our lives in a new way.

Forgiveness

Let us now try to bring all this yet a little closer to home. It brings enormous relief to realise that we do not have to go through life carrying our burden of guilt. When God deals with the sin problem he takes no half measures. When he says, 'It is OK', anything you may have done (and every wrong act you will commit in the future) is completely taken care of. It's gone. That is not a poetic hyperbole but expresses a glorious reality. 'Who is a God like you,' the prophet Micah asked, 'who pardons sins and forgives the transgression? . . . You will tread our sins underfoot and hurl all our iniquities into the sea.'[101]

God has a selective memory. Time and again we are told that he will not forget us. He remembers us as persons, as people who belong to him (if that is what we want!) But once we have asked him to forgive our sins, he does so, because our sins have been dealt with, once and for all. And then he will no longer remember those sins. Speaking of the rebellious conduct of ancient Israel, God made a promise which just as certainly applies to Americans and Germans, Dutch and Filipinos, and you name it, of today: 'I will forgive their wickedness and will remember their sins no more!'[102]

What a decisive difference there is between God and us. We easily forget the people around us as persons who may need our care, but tend to have a frightening capacity to remember how people have failed us. If people have treated us unkindly or have been unfair in what they did or said, we tend to remember this, sometimes for the rest of our lives. But that is not what God does. He remembers us as individuals who are dear to him; we are eternally safe in his memory, but he will not give another thought to any of our sins. They are forgiven! God took care of all the wrongs we ever did and shall do when Jesus Christ died on the cross, and this 'mystery of grace' made provision for our eternal well-being.

Now, there may be some who read this, who feel that this is too good to be true. They may feel that their life is such that they simply cannot believe that they are included in this 'mystery' (or should I say: miracle) of grace. If that is how you feel, stop right here, get a Bible off the shelf and find the section indicated as Luke 15:11-31 (and if you do not consider yourself as being in this category, you would also do well to read it, for it will reinforce your faith in the 'mystery of grace.' It is one of the most moving stories of the Bible). Read it and you will get the point!

I earlier used the expression: No strings attached. I need to qualify that. For receiving forgiveness from God must be coupled to a readiness on our part to forgive other people. It is an important theme in the model prayer that Jesus once taught his apprentices: 'Forgive us our debts, as we have also forgiven our debtors.'[103] This may not come easy, but there is no way around it. The divine forgiveness that is offered to us, totally free, presupposes our willingness to forgive the people around us. Not once or twice, but without limit. When someone once asked Jesus how often one should forgive, he answered: seventy-seven times![104] That is the string that is attached!

We need God's forgiveness, but other people also need our forgiveness. Philip Yancey, a popular Christian author who has the ability to make complex subjects crystal clear, retells in his book *What's So Amazing About Grace?* a story that we owe to Hemingway. It is about a man in Spain who had long been estranged from his son. He began to feel guilty about the way in which he had dealt with his son and wanted to re-establish contact with him. In order to find him he placed an add in a Madrid newspaper. The text of the advertisement was: 'Paco, everything is forgiven. Meet me next Tuesday in Hotel Montana at 12 pm.' When the father went to the hotel, his son was there. But there were also another 800 young men who answered to the name Paco![105] Yes, lots of people are looking for forgiveness!

It may not always be easy to forgive or to ask for forgiveness. The 'eye for an eye' approach is often more natural to us. Human nature tends to think in terms of vendettas, retaliation or, at the very least, compensation. But that is not the way of God and can no longer be ours once we have caught a glimpse of the 'mystery of God's grace.'

Chapter six

Rest

In July 1997 I was on one of my regular trips from the United Kingdom to the United States. I cannot recall whether it was on the way going or when coming back. But I remember that I found the movie totally uninteresting and had finished the spy novel I had in my hand luggage. So, out of sheer boredom I picked up the in-flight magazine, which I rarely ever touch. But before too long I saw an article with the intriguing title *Ancient Wisdom*. The by-line told me it was written by Nan Chase, 'a frequent contributor to the *Washington Post*.' I began to read and to my surprise it turned out to be about the immense benefits of the Saturday-Sabbath. I kept reading because the topic happens to be of great interest to me since I belong to one of the few Christian denominations that have chosen to have their weekly day of rest and worship on the Saturday rather than on the Sunday. This is what she wrote:

'Not so long ago I was just another harried working mom, rushing through the day with one thought always in mind: Why isn't there any time?

'Then, in a moment of divine inspiration, I decided to try an old-fashioned cure for my Space Age blues. It's called the Sabbath, and it's a mental health tool that works as well today as it did 3,200 years ago when the Hebrews codified a weekly day of rest as the Fourth Commandment. . . .

'My personal life, my professional life, and my family life have all improved, and I plan to go on celebrating the Sabbath. The most powerful and illuminating discovery for me may be the sudden understanding of how an ancient edict can have such thoroughly modern applications; Sabbath began thousands of years ago as the answer to the burdens of ceaseless and difficult labour. . . . [Today] our problems aren't all that different. . . .

'I look forward to my weekly holiday. As the sun goes down each Friday evening, I take off my wristwatch, and for a night and a day time stands still.'[106]

Take any book on postmodernism and you will discover that one of the key attitudes of postmodern people towards religion is that they want to know what it *does* for them. That interests them far more than the question whether the fine points of a particular doctrine are true and can be 'proven' from the Bible. *Experience* is far higher on their list of values than the *theory* of religion. If they have an interest in religion (and many have) they are looking for relevancy. Well, if ever there was a feature of the Christian faith that it is still relevant – or more relevant than ever – it is the weekly day of rest as prescribed in the Bible. Life in the twenty-first century demands that we have time off on a regular basis if we are going to survive with our full humanity intact.

We need rest

Until a year or so ago I had little idea what was meant by the term burn-out. I have never experienced it and hope I never will. When, from time to time, I heard about people who were diagnosed with that problem, I was inclined to think that most of it was down to 'something between the ears'. I must admit that I tended to think that such people should not exaggerate things and should just pull themselves together. After all, who does not feel exhausted from time to time? A bit of positive thinking, a few long walks in the woods or along the beach, and a week on the Canary Islands or in Bermuda would, I thought, go a long way to remedy the situation. That was what I believed until I took the time to read a book which chronicles the burn-out of a pastor who worked in a mid-size church in a rural part of the Netherlands. I know the area well and it seemed unlikely to me this could be the setting for much stress. But this autobiography of a burn-out pastor made me understand how serious such a situation can be, how it can arise and the havoc it can cause for an individual and for his family.[107]

Burn-out is only one of the many ways in which our turbo-charged existence can become derailed. Stress is a normal phenomenon and a certain amount of it is good for us. But it is not normal to become so stressed out that you completely lose your joy of living and feel that you are constantly chasing something that always remains just beyond your reach. It is not acceptable that you feel constantly under a terrible pressure to do things, ever more things, and to do them ever better. Even children suffer from stress as – often because of unrealistic parental expectations – they have to rush from school to music lessons and from there to the sports club, and then back to do homework in preparation for the school work of the following day. They must be cute and clever. Countless women are stressed out as they try to juggle the demands of their full time job with their 'duties' at home, since even in these days of gender equality most of the cooking, washing, ironing and cleaning is still very much a female 'prerogative'. Heart disease used to be a male problem. But gender equality has also been introduced into that area of life (and death).

Among men stress is not reserved for the top brass of the business world. Also in the ranks of higher and middle management the latest, ever more powerful, laptop travels between work and home, and e-mail does not stop coming in when office work on Friday afternoon ends. The mobile phone is switched on during evenings and during the weekend, and the taboo on letting business-related matters intrude into private time and space has long been disregarded by many companies. In fact many businesses have an unwritten rule that employees above a certain level ought to be contactable at almost any time. Stress, chronic fatigue, depression, burn-out, high blood pressure and stomach ulcers have become common fixtures of present-day life. To be a workaholic is considered by many as being plain stupid, but for countless others it is the price they are prepared to pay to get ahead in their professional life.

The tempo of Western life has, strangely enough, steadily increased over the past few decades. I remember predictions that our working week would continue to shorten as more and more of our work would be taken over by machines and computers. For a while it seemed that this optimistic prediction would come true. Annual holidays became longer, most people got a five-day working week, and in many sectors of industry the number of working hours a week fell to below forty. In Europe, in particular, the numbers of people taking early retirement grew dramatically. In some countries people quit their job on the average at age 58. But all of this is changing. Partly, this has to do with the economic situation. In many 'rich' countries labour costs have to be reduced in order to stay competitive, and one way of doing that is to have fewer people work more hours for the same amount of money. Also, less money is available to make early retirement of large numbers of people possible. But there are also other factors.

The computer was supposed to make things easier for us. And in many ways it has done so. But the new technology has also created a rapidly growing demand for more information and far more detailed reporting. It has also shifted a lot of work. There was a time when I dictated my letters to a secretary who would take notes in shorthand, and all I had to do then was to sign the finished product. Later I started using a dictaphone and my secretary would receive her daily batch of small tapes to process, before the finished letters would come back to me for my signature. Now I mostly type my own e-mails and when I decide to write a 'real' letter, I tend to write a draft on my computer, which I then send in digital form to my secretary. Some time ago I finally learnt how to use the PowerPoint programme. Indeed, it enhances my presentations, but it does require considerable extra time. I also tend to book my own travel on the Internet, whereas in the past my secretary would work things out with the travel agent. And, as I travel, I do not just make the occasional phone call to the office to find out whether everything is all right, but I keep current with my e-mail. The first thing I now do when entering a hotel room is not to investigate the quality of the bed, but I first look for ways to access my e-mail and the Internet. And so, life gets busier all the time.

As our standard of living has gone up, so has the amount of DIY that comes our way. There is always something to change or improve somewhere in the house or in the garden. We are supposed to have more time for our hobbies and other recreational activities than our parents had in the past. But somehow these things have become more complicated and many approach these 'free' time activities with a passion that looks far too much like hard work. And even though many people start wishing us a 'good weekend' from Thursday afternoon onwards, it seems that to a great many people the weekend brings very little actual rest and recreation.

There are, however, numerous signals that change is in the air. And that has clearly to do with the onset of postmodern thinking. Attitudes to work have begun to change. It is dawning on an increasing number of, mainly young, people that there is more to life than work. They do not want to take their work home and to think about it during the weekend. Many consciously choose to forego a promotion and higher salary in order to avoid responsibilities they do not want, and they object to a life that is all work. An increasing number of couples deliberately choose to have a part-time job each, so that even though this means they will have less money and may not be able to buy a house in the most expensive area of town, they will have more quality time for themselves and for the things that really matter to them.

In recent years a plethora of books has come on the market and many seminars are offered that emphasize the need of taking stock of where we are going and the benefits of slowing down. They present detailed instructions as to how one might do so. Many companies and institutions are more and more conscious of the need to provide employees with sabbaticals – a few months every few years during which their workers can recharge their batteries as they study or travel, or work on a special project. And there is an increasing number of people who leave their jobs for six months or a year and take off to some far away place, doing something completely different from what they used to do, before returning to a new assignment refreshed and with a new motivation and new energy levels.

People are increasingly realizing they need rest. They sense there is more to life than work, success, money, status, and ambitions. But, sadly enough, they often fail to access a source of rest that is unparalleled in its scope and effectiveness. It is primarily spiritual in nature. 'Come to me, you who are burdened and weary, and I will give you rest.'[108] These are words spoken by Jesus Christ. But though they were uttered almost two thousand years ago, it was not a temporary proposition. The offer is still valid. Another New Testament statement underlines that the offer of this rest has never been withdrawn: 'There remains, then, a Sabbath rest for the people of God.'[109]

Time set aside

It is no coincidence that in the Bible verse we just quoted this ongoing offer of rest is connected with the concept of the Sabbath, a day of rest once every seven days. We are so used to the fact that our time is parcelled out in years, months, weeks and days that we do not stop very often to think about why this is so. Of course, if we do, we recognize that the length of the *year*, the *month* and the *day* respectively is based on the movement of the earth around the sun, the movement of the moon around the earth and the turning of the earth around its axis. But where does the *week* come from? Various theories have been proposed. Historians have suggested that somewhere in the ancient world a market day that was held once every seven days may have been at the origin of the weekly cycle, or that the week was derived from some ancient Kenite or Babylonian feast day that came in a seven-day cycle. And several other hypotheses have been put forward, but none of these has been really convincing.[110] It makes much more sense to stay with the explanation given on the first pages of the Bible, where God is portrayed as the Creator of heaven and earth. Time was then sliced up into segments of seven-day weeks. Each week would have six days for *work* and one day – the seventh – for *rest*. This is how it is stated:

'Thus the heavens and earth were completed in all their vast array. By the seventh day he finished the work he had been doing; so on the seventh day he rested from all his work. And God blessed the seventh day and made it holy, because on it he rested from all the work of creating he had done.'[111]

Among the important messages the first chapters of the Bible deliver to us, is the assertion that two institutions are literally as old as mankind: marriage and the seventh-day rest. Apparently it was the intention of the great Designer-God that these two institutions would be woven into the fabric of human life. Looking in the Bible for further information on the history of one of those institutions – the Sabbath – we find an interesting story in the sixteenth chapter of Exodus, the second book of the Bible. As the name of that section indicates, it deals with the events connected with the migration of the descendents of Abraham away from their 400-year slavery in northern Egypt. During the forty years of their sojourn in the Sinai desert, before they were able to enter the land that was to be theirs, God miraculously provided for food. As he did so, he taught them a lesson about the seventh-day Sabbath through the manner in which he scheduled the delivery of this food. Adequate daily rations were provided on days one to five, but on day six there was a double portion, so that no food collection and distribution needed to take place on the seventh day – the day of rest!

When God provided the Law of the Ten Commandments (Exodus 20:8), the ten basic principles for human life that we already encountered in the previous chapter which give a prominent place to the seventh-day Sabbath, this was not an unexpected novelty but a *reiteration* of a long-standing principle that, unfortunately, had been seriously neglected by those who should have practised it. This regrettable fact is implied in the first word of this fourth commandment: *Remember!*

'*Remember* the Sabbath day by keeping it holy. Six days you shall labour and do all your work, but the seventh day is a Sabbath to the Lord your God. On it you shall not do any work. Neither you, nor your son, or daughter, nor your manservant or maidservant, nor your animals, nor the aliens within your gates. For in six days the Lord made the heavens and the earth, the sea, and all that is in them, but he rested on the seventh day.

Therefore the Lord *blessed* the Sabbath day and *made it holy*.'

A study of the word 'remember', as used in the Bible, reveals that it is pregnant with meaning. 'Remembering' is not merely a matter of using our memory. In this particular message it tells us to focus on the crucial message that is to follow. It can be taken as a series of exclamation marks: Note!!! What follows is of utmost importance!

Keep the Sabbath *holy*. Make it into a day that remains separate from the other six; a day that is different and will stand out among the days of the week. Don't try to improve on a perfect system and do not fiddle with it. The French tried to do so in the time of Napoleon. They tried to do away with the seven day week and replaced the week with units of ten days. They put an enormous effort into enforcing this alteration, but they did not succeed. It simply did not work, and after a few years the experiment was discontinued. No other serious attempt has been made to do away with the week, but there is a more subtle way in which a calendar modification has been introduced. Many calendars and diaries have made what used to be the first day of the week into the seventh day, while making the seventh day into the sixth. (We shall see that this adjustment is not as innocuous as it may appear.)

Remember to keep that special day *holy*, the commandment says. There are things we can do to fulfil that commandment. But we can only *keep* it holy because it *is* holy. *We* do not make the day holy, but the key thing to remember is *that God has made it holy*.

What is involved in keeping holy what God made holy?

'Setting aside a holy Sabbath means that we cease our productivity and accomplishments for one day in every seven. The exciting thing about such a practice is that it changes our attitudes for the rest of the week. It frees us up to worry less about how much we produce on the other days. Furthermore, when we end that futile chasing after the wind, we can truly rest and learn delight in new ways.'[112]

We must note that there is a direct link between the Sabbath and the creation of the world. Every Sabbath we interrupt our own frantic activities and shift our focus to the fact that God is the Creator of everything, and concentrate on all that this important insight implies. Recognizing oneself as a created being leads to the realization that one owes a worshipful response to the Creator. It reinforces in a powerful way the feeling of the absolute creature-Creator dependency we discussed when we took the first steps in our journey of discovery. It gives the meaning to our lives that we crave. It corrects the arrogant, but completely ill-informed view that man is the measure of all things. He is not, for God as the Creator lays out the measuring stick against which our goals and deepest motives must be measured.

The recognition that everything in this world is created and owes its ultimate existence to the grand Designer, not only changes our relationship to fellow human beings, but also to non-human creatures and the resources of our world. It conflicts with the 'modern' notion that man can exploit Planet Earth as he sees fit. In many ways this selfish exploitation of the treasures of our world, which was part of the 'modern' mindset that believed in incessant progress, is continuing even today (very much to the benefit of the rich countries). But the postmodern person has understood that this approach will eventually lead to global disaster and pleads for a far more careful management of the dwindling resources and a responsible custody of our fragile ecosystems. This very much fits in with the biblical idea that as created beings we need to act responsibly towards the other elements of God's creation. After all, everything that exists is his, and we are only caretakers on his behalf. Against this backdrop the seventh-day Sabbath, which points to creation, is a potent weekly reminder of our true status and our fundamental relationship to the world around us.

Having said that, we also need to look at another basic aspect of our 'remembering' to keep the Sabbath day holy. When discussing the Sabbath commandment we usually refer to the version we find in Exodus 20, as we did above. But there is also a slightly different version of the Ten Commandments in the book of Deuteronomy, and there we find an additional motivation for keeping the seventh day 'holy'. The weekly Sabbath is also a commemoration of Israel's delivery from the Egyptian bondage, and thus, by extension, of every kind of slavery from which God's grace has set us free.

The slavery of our times takes many forms. One of the most pernicious kinds of present-day slavery is that of the clock and the calendar. Many of us have also become slaves to such things as computers and mobile phones. We often find it incredibly difficult to separate work time from leisure time. It seems that modern life requires that we can at all times instantly switch into our work-mode. The Sabbath is the perfect antidote to this type of bondage which threatens every form of true rest, both physical and spiritual. The words of Old Testament scholar Jon Dybdahl ring very true:

'If there is any command hurried and hassled modern people need, it is the Sabbath. We are so busy trying to create meaning in our own time and serving ourselves that we forget that God is the only One who can give meaning to our lives. We show our "resting" in him by resting on his day.'[113]

How do we rest?

The prophet Isaiah admonished the people of his day to take the keeping of the Sabbath seriously. This is what he said:

'If you keep your feet from *breaking* the Sabbath
  and from doing *as you please* on my holy day,
if you call the Sabbath a *delight* and the Lord's
  holy day honourable,
and if you *honour* it by not *going your own way*
  and not doing as you please or speaking idle words,
then you will find your *joy* in the Lord,
  and I will cause you to ride on the heights of the land
and to *feast on the inheritance* of your father Jacob.'
(Isaiah 58:13.)

Postmodern people might suggest that this statement needs some 'deconstruction'. Indeed, what does it mean in today's language? What did Isaiah mean and what can it mean for us when we read it in the early years of the twenty-first century? I have italicised a few key words. There is apparently a form of behaviour that is defined as 'breaking' the Sabbath, i.e. failing to observe it in the intended way. A few lines further down, this is referred to as 'going your own way.' That means: making yourself the focus of the day, as you do when you take a day off to go to an amusement park or when you decide to spend the day at a beauty farm. Or when all that matters to you on that day is how you yourself feel, and how you can simply withdraw into your own private world. Instead, the intentional focal point is on 'honouring' the day by recognizing its true value, 'remembering' its link to all of God's creation, and escaping from all that curtails your inner freedom. And note: That does not make this day a dreary day, full of restrictions, but the 'holy' day, that is different from all other days; it becomes a 'delight', a 'joy', and a 'feast'.

Yes, but how does that translate in actual life? Is there a model which can show us how this can 'work' for us? I know of people who do their level best to 'keep' the Sabbath holy. They make a detailed inventory of things they feel are conducive to protecting the holiness of that day and decide in great detail which things may hinder them in safeguarding its unique nature. Maybe – just maybe – this is something that works for them, but I am totally convinced that such lists cannot provide a satisfying model for others to follow, let alone that it should be *forced* upon others. I have travelled around the world enough to realize that such regulations are often more a reflection of culture and tradition than of a clear understanding of the Bible.

I am sceptical about making lists of specific do's and don'ts, because they underemphasize the importance of underlying attitudes and motives. The danger of a lifeless, legalistic approach to the day of rest – of reducing the joy of that holy day to a set of mechanical rules and regulations – is very real and a remains a constant and ever present danger. It destroys the joy of Christian living because it operates from a fear of always falling short of the ideal. It is based on the erroneous assumption that we may earn our salvation by our good behaviour. Sabbath keeping which is motivated by a desire to earn extra brownie points that can be recorded on the credit side of our eternal account, will inevitably be a burden rather than a blessing and a delight.

'The God who made the Sabbath is not a cranky schoolmaster, always forbidding, coercing obedience, and watching sniveling subjects slinking into cowardly compliance. The Sabbath commandment comes from a kind, wise teacher who does not like to see us suffer. "Let me make it easier for you," God says. "Some things may seem expedient, or important, or profitable – but in the end, they will bring you suffering. If you work all week and forget to rest, you will become brittle and hard, and lose precious nourishment and joy. Forgetting the Sabbath is like forgetting to unwrap the most beautiful gift under the tree." '[114]

Obviously, if we are to enjoy the rest of the Sabbath we must be intentional in removing any obstacles and must make some conscious decisions as to what will help us or hinder us in receiving God's rest. However, rather than looking for a definitive model among contemporaries who have discovered the divine gift of the Sabbath, we should look at how Jesus Christ modelled the keeping of the Sabbath. He squarely rejected the legalism that was an endemic problem among his compatriots, and underlined a basic principle: The Sabbath was made for man, not man for the Sabbath.[115] In other words, in arranging for this weekly instalment of holy time, man's interests were at the forefront. God does not just want to make a point in terms of 'Do as I say, or else', but rather in terms of, 'Please, do as I say and you will see how your life will be enriched.'

Part of Jesus' enjoyment of the weekly Sabbath was his interaction with others at the local synagogue (roughly the Jewish equivalent for what Christians today call church). It was his 'custom' to do so.[116] Being together with other believers in the setting of prayer, reading from the Bible, religious instruction and meditation helps us to focus on our relationship with God, to reinforce that basic feeling of absolute dependence, and to sustain the leaps of faith that we discussed. But Jesus did not spend the entire Sabbath in the synagogue. I urge you to find and read a few of the passages in the story of Jesus' life that took place on the seventh day of the week.[117] You will find Jesus walking in nature. You will find him socializing with his friends. And you will find him involved in activities to help people in need. You will also discover that he refused to be bound by petty rules that others tried to force upon him. Furthermore, it is not by accident that he died on a Friday (the sixth day) and was resurrected on the Sunday (the first day), and 'rested' in the tomb on the Sabbath (the seventh day). In his life and in his death he was the ultimate Model that continues to inspire us in our quest for genuine rest.

Physical rest is most definitely included in this Sabbath rest. Sleeping in for a few hours on the day of rest is not a sin. In fact, it might be a good idea to rethink the times of some church meetings, so that church goers do not have to hurry so much as they get ready for church. (After all, the traditional 10am time was based on the fact that the cows needed to be milked before their owners could go to church, and not on any lofty Bible-based principle.) The luxury of taking a nap for about an hour after the mid-day lunch on Sabbath is something I must admit I enjoy immensely. And there are, of course, many other ways that may involve a bit more physical energy but which nonetheless help us to unwind.

Physical relaxation is, however, only part of the Sabbath package. It also very much includes rest from the worries of everyday life, from dealing with difficult issues and controversies, and – I would suggest – an intentional distancing oneself for twenty-four hours from the constant information bombardment through the various media. It is a time, as Nan Chase said in the beginning of this chapter, to take our watches off and let the time stand still! Let me quote once again from Marva Dawn's book to underline this important point:

'Perhaps the most important aspect of Sabbath keeping that contributes immensely to wholeness in our human existence is the prevalence of order. We crave order to give us a sense that things are under control, that we can cope with whatever might be happening because it fits into a larger plan. That is why the keeping of the Sabbath rhythm is so important: the orderly cycle of six days of work and one day of resting and embracing God's values matches the rhythm of our creation which God has revealed to us in the Scriptures. . . .

'To keep the Sabbath means to cherish it, to honour it as the Queen of our days, in consort with the King of the Universe. To develop the habit of Sabbath keeping requires some intentionality on our part, but ultimately sets us free from any sort of legalism.

Its ordering sets us free to be creative. Its ceasing enables us to rest; its feasting enables us to embrace afresh.'[118]

What or when?

The reality is that most Christians are Sunday keepers (first day of the week) rather than Sabbath keepers (seventh day). Does that make a significant difference? Many would say, 'Surely, nothing is wrong with that, as long as we stick to the basic idea of keeping one day in seven holy.' Two things need to be said in response to this. Firstly, most Sunday keepers do not actually treat their day of rest in a way that even resembles the kind of Sabbath keeping described above, and thus by this fact alone they miss out on the tremendous benefits of the Sabbath. And, secondly, we should 'remember' that it was not the first day of the week but the *seventh* that God decided to make 'holy.' There is no way we can arbitrarily change this. To say that God's timetable does not really matter is arrogant to say the least.

'The Sabbath is a powerful testimony to the sovereignty of God. Only he can create, and only he can make something holy. This is why Adventists so strongly object to the change from Sabbath to Sunday as the Christian day of rest and worship. Without a clear mandate, such a development is nothing less than an affront to God.'[119]

Indeed, today Seventh-day Adventists hold a minority position among Christians in their commitment to the seventh-day Sabbath.[120] Throughout the centuries, however, it is not only the Jews who have stuck with the biblical day of rest, but also Christians of various persuasions. It is widely recognized by scholars that it was a human decision to exchange the Sabbath for the Sunday as the day of rest and worship. Many factors were involved in the process that led to the change. In some countries the change was made in the early centuries of the church's history, while in other areas it took hundreds of additional years before the transition was complete. Anti-Semitism and the fear of showing too much similarity with the Jews was an important factor.[121] When, in the sixteenth century, the church split into a Roman Catholic branch and a Reformation branch, the debate about the issue flared up and some groups opted once again for the Sabbath. Today, Seventh-day Adventists are the largest – but not the only – Christian community that stresses the special blessings of the day which God, rather than any human individual or institution, has declared 'holy'.

Seventh-day Adventists will make sure that when they talk about the day of rest the dialogue does not only focus on whether it is on the *first* day of the week or on the *seventh*. For, even more than in the past, the very concept of a 'holy' day that is set aside from the rest of our time and is in some sense 'special', has been lost and must be reintroduced in the minds of the people.

The specificity about the seventh-day which we find in the fourth of the Ten Commandments is something we should not lose sight of. When God provides guidelines for human happiness, it is not a matter of pick and choose, or of adaptation according to our personal preferences. James, one of the apostles we have not quoted from so far, tends to be very direct in his comments. He says: If you ignore one of these principles (the context makes it clear that he refers to the Ten Commandments), you might as well ignore all of them.[122] Somehow, the seventh-day Sabbath appears to be a kind of test case as to whether or not we are serious about living in harmony with God's intentions for us and fully appreciative of the design of creation. When God prepared the miraculous food (as we saw earlier in this chapter), he was very specific about the timing of its arrival. He said, 'In this I will *test* them.'[123] Referring back to the giving of the Ten Commandments, God said, via the prophet Ezekiel, 'I gave them my Sabbaths as a *sign* between us [i.e. between the people and me], so that they would know that I the Lord made them holy.'[124] 'Holy' people – those who are 'separate' and different because of their desire to live in ultimate dependence on their Designer-God – will keep the 'holy' day of God as a sign of their loyalty to him.

In the last section of the Bible, the Book of Revelation, we are given a grand panorama through the ages of the struggle between good and evil. The theme moves back and forth as it describes the various players in highly symbolic language, but it always returns to the eventual victory of good over evil. The final phase of earth's history is going to be a challenging time for those who want openly to confess their faith in God. What will characterise these people who will cling to their faith in spite of all the pressures to turn their backs on God? The last book of the Bible makes the point that this minority will continue to anchor the meaning of life in their faith in God and will stick to the eternal principles of the Ten Commandments.[125]

When you give this some further thought, it appears logical that the fourth commandment will continue to serve as a test, similar to the way it functioned in the Old Testament period. In a recent book in which he explains what the Bible says about the phase of history just prior to the return of Jesus Christ, Jon Paulien points out how all ten commandments 'are reasonable and even contain a certain amount of self-interest.' Then he makes this significant statement:

'The one part of the Ten Commandments that is not "logical" is the command to worship on Saturday rather than on some other day. Such a command is so lacking in logic and self-interest that secular people find it easy to ignore. After all, no one has been able to demonstrate scientifically a significant difference between Saturday and any other day of the week. The sun shines and the rain falls in the usual amounts. The earth continues to spin and revolve around the sun. The only difference between Saturday and other days is that God himself made a distinction between them. To keep the Sabbath is to take God at his word in spite of the fact that the five senses can perceive no evidence that to do so is reasonable. It is this very "irrelevance" that makes the Sabbath an ideal test of loyalty at the end.'[126]

This chapter does not demand a leap of faith of the magnitude that was necessary in the previous chapters. The present chapter deals with something that can be directly experienced in the here and now by all who give it a serious try. In spite of all the books we read about time management and all the seminars about this topic we may attend, 'most of us lack a genuine Christian perspective on our attitude towards and our use of time.'[127] As a result we miss out on the kind of rest that can make a dramatic difference in the way we live and experience our faith and our relationships. We can do so alone, or together with others. Joining others will increase our blessings further. If you want to know more about this, just keep on reading.

Chapter seven

Community

In this chapter I will dare to suggest that attending church and belonging to a church community is a good idea. I am sure at least some readers will say, 'Wait a minute. Where have you been for the last twenty years? If you had been paying attention, you would have noticed that the church in the Western world has stopped being a going concern. The church is in deep trouble. It often does not seem to know what it believes. It is hit by disgusting moral scandals. It does not have the kind of financial and political clout it once possessed. It is harder than ever to find people who sense a calling to become a minister or priest. And church attendance goes in one direction: down and further down.'

I hear this all the time. I am not blind to what is happening. But this picture is not totally accurate and is not as alarming as it is made out to be, as we shall see. There is no question, however, that the institutional church has hit more than just a few patches of rough weather. And this has not gone unnoticed by those who study ecclesiastical trends. Two shelves in my modest library are occupied with books that deal with the lamentable 'state of the church', and with the need for change if the church is to survive. Most of these books offer statistics that leave little to the imagination and make the reader wonder: Who will be the man (or more likely: woman) to switch off the light in the church for the last time? Writing about the 'death of the church', Mike Regele says that 'we must not dismiss the possibility that our human structures, our human institutions pass into history.' If there is no drastic change, he continues, 'the church as we have known it will be crushed in the seismic waves of change that are rattling our lives.'[128]

I am convinced, however, that in spite of all the predictions to the contrary, the church has a future. The church of the future may differ in many ways from the traditional kind of institution that most of us associate with the word 'church', but there will be a church. Why can I be so sure? It is because the church is not a human invention. Many of its traditional structures and embellishments may be temporal, but the concept of a community of believers, who are part of a visible 'body' of people, and all share in the same convictions and ideals, will not disappear.

Alone or together?

Before we try to define in more detail what we mean when we use the word 'church', we must look at a few more general, but very basic, facets. When we analyze the social behaviour of contemporary people we get a confusing and rather paradoxical picture. On the one hand, we notice a trend towards isolation and cocooning. Large numbers of people prefer to live alone. Intentionally. We are assured that we do not need to feel sorry for them, for this is what they want. They do everything to protect the privacy of their own world. A good weekend is a forty-eight-hour period of remaining indoors, sleeping in, ordering a pizza, watching some DVDs, listening to music, and surfing the Internet. But at the same time, there seems to be an overwhelming, and almost universal, need to be in touch with other people. The telecommunication companies earn their billions as people chat for hours at a time, use their mobile phones wherever they are, and send their innumerable SMS messages. They enjoy being engulfed by the crowds at rock festivals and carnivals, and being jam-packed together with hundreds or thousands of other people in discotheques and sports arenas. Most of these things have no great attraction to me personally. But I must admit that, when I lived in the UK, I got somewhat infected with the very special atmosphere during the Last Night of the Proms in a crammed and exuberant Royal Albert Hall. And when I lived in West Africa, meeting my fellow Dutch expatriates in the embassy on the Queen's birthday and singing our national anthem together, was something I did not want to miss.

Although there is this need on the part of most of us to have space and time for ourselves and to be alone, away from all and everything, there is very clearly also an urgent need to be together with people, to share with others in the joys and griefs that come our way. Men and women in the twenty-first century Western world continue to be social beings, just as their parents and grandparents were. People network more than ever before, and they continue to yearn for friendships and relationships. People want to celebrate together. They want to mourn together. Most of us feel sorry for 'loners', who are unable to socialize and make friends. Our intuition tells us that children miss out on something important if they spend most of their time alone, playing computer games or surfing the net, without having other children around them. We also realize that we usually need the support and encouragement of other people if we want to achieve some substantial goals. Most people who suffer from a severe physical handicap or struggle against certain ugly habits or addictions benefit from associating with people who are faced with similar problems. This phenomenon explains the success of such organizations as *Alcoholics Anonymous* and *Weight Watchers*, and the massive interest in numerous support groups for people with Alzheimer's, diabetes, cancer, and so on.

Why should it be different when it comes to our spiritual life? Certainly, there are aspects of our inner life that belong to the 'inside'. There are thoughts we will only share with our Maker. There are times when we do not need or want the presence of others, but prefer the stillness of a quiet space at home or the serenity of a small chapel in a cathedral. We treasure the unexpected moments when we feel an ultimate dependence on the

Beyond in some special, unmediated, way and realize that we are part of something larger than ourselves.

But it is of the very essence of faith that it is experienced in community with others; that believers support one another in their journey of discovery and share their faith with one another and with the outside world. True, there always were individuals who lived alone, in complete isolation from others, but who nonetheless remained true to their faith. Thousands upon thousands, through the centuries, have entered convents or monasteries, in search of a life of prayer and contemplation, far away from the buzz of everyday life. In most cases, these people looked for a special kind of community. Some, however, opted for total isolation. However much respect one may have for such immense dedication towards an ideal, one can hardly say that this is the kind of life that Christ modeled to his followers. Yes, he went into the desert for a forty-day retreat and occasionally wanted complete solitude for a brief period of time[129], but his life, in general, was spent in the midst of a community of followers and in the company of friends and often large groups of people.

The ultimate support group

The previous chapters dealt with the good news that God exists and has revealed to us what we need to do to find meaning in our lives through a series of leaps of faith. But the journey of discovery continues. God knows that most of us crave for community – for that's how he designed us. Right from the very beginning he determined that it would not be good for humans to be alone.[130] He knew that they would need and enjoy company. That's why he made us as males and females and gave us the possibility to procreate. And that is why, later in human history, he created the people of Israel. It was to be a people with a mission in the world of antiquity. Their assignment was to convince other peoples they came in contact with that the living Designer-God, who is the Creator of everything, is infinitely superior to the lifeless artefacts that are often worshipped as 'gods.' They had a sanctuary – a place of worship where they would assemble at regular intervals, to celebrate their feasts and to give expression to their faith in the God who had shown his hand so clearly in their personal and corporate history.

Christians have had differing views on the role of Israel in God's plan after the birth of the church. In the first chapters of the book of Acts we see how the first Christians preached the resurrection of Christ to the Jews as something that fulfilled 'the Law and the Prophets', while still sharing in the traditional temple and synagogue services. And the apostle Paul teaches about God's continued efforts to save Israel.[131] But, having said that, it is also clear that Jesus began something new. For example, during his last meal with his disciples he established a 'new covenant' based on his death.[132] It is also clear that he selected and trained a company of followers whom he authorized and sent out to the world with a mission.[133]

In retrospect we can only wonder in sheer amazement how a small band of unsophisticated people could become the powerful nucleus of a movement that soon would reach the entire Mediterranean world, and even regions far beyond, with the message of the One whom they knew was risen from the grave. People in what is now Palestine, Syria, Lebanon, Greece, Cyprus and Malta, North Africa and even India – and many other places – banded together in groups. For quite some time they met in private houses and public places before they built church buildings with baptisteries in which the new members could be immersed as a public sign of their entrance into the church.

From the very beginning these groups of believers were organized. They soon agreed to statements that summarized the main tenets of their faith. They met together for prayer, the reading of the Bible (the Old Testament and the new writings that were to become the New Testament, and which soon began to circulate). A number of rituals were established. Gradually the new movement found is own identity and the members wanted to be known as 'Christians'.[134] Over time it ceased to be a Jewish sect.

The story of the earliest phase of the history of the church is told in the book of the Bible that is called *Acts* of the Apostles. You can read the twenty-eight chapters in a few hours. It is a fascinating account. It takes you from Jerusalem to Rome, and all over the ancient world. If your Bible has some maps in the back, look at them and study, in particular, the missionary journeys of the apostle Paul. As you begin to read, pay special attention to chapter two, where you will find the amazing story of what happened in Jerusalem just fifty days after Jesus had risen from the dead, and ten days after he had left this earth. Pilgrims from far and near had assembled in Jerusalem for Pentecost, one the great annual feasts of the Jews. They spoke a wide array of languages, which posed a tremendous problem to Jesus' followers who wanted to spread the news of what had happened to their Master. Then, somehow, God solved the communication crisis and made it possible for everyone to hear what the apostles had to say in his own language or dialect. Professor Richard Rice's comment is very much to the point: 'The story of Pentecost underlines the fact that the church is not a human creation, but it owes its existence to the power of God.' This leads to his further conclusion which I wholeheartedly underline, 'That church, then, is a community which human beings cannot produce. What happens among members of the church, the spirit of fellowship which they enjoy, is something only the unique presence of God can explain.'[135] Let's look at this in more detail.

What does the word 'church' mean?

Ask people in the street what they think the term 'church' means and they will most likely point to a building or to an organization. The Notre Dame in Paris, Westminster Abbey in London and the National Cathedral in Washington are 'churches'. The Roman Catholic Church, the Baptist Church and the Lutheran Church are 'churches'. No doubt, these usages of the word 'church' have been validated by their long tradition over the centuries. We use the word to distinguish between 'secular' buildings, mosques and synagogues, and buildings for Christian worship. The term is also quite useful when we distinguish between the many branches of the Christian faith. There are thousands of different Christian denominations – no one knows, in fact, exactly how many there are – and they are commonly referred to as either churches or sects. The term 'sect' has, however, acquired the rather negative connotation of a group of people which majors on minors and/or tends to be extreme in its beliefs and behaviour. No doubt, this can become rather subjective, but the point is that most Christian denominations like to be referred to as a 'church.'

We would, however, search in vain if we were looking for that explanation of the term 'church' in the Bible. The biblical root meaning of the Greek *ekklesia* has nothing to do with bricks and mortar or legal organizations, but has to do with *people*. It is based upon two Greek words: *ek* and *kalein*, which translate as 'out of' and 'to call.' The word *church,* and also its collaterals in many other languages, such as Iglesia (Spanish), Chiesa (Italian), Kirche (German), Kirke (Scottish, Danish, Norwegian), Kyrka (Swedish), Kerk (Dutch), etc., thus literally means: 'Those who are called out.' 'Church' is the label for those who have been 'called out' from the 'world' (i.e. from a life without faith in Christ) to a life within the community of faith in Christ. It is a community of people in a particular location, which recognizes itself as being 'called' by God. Amazingly, within decades after Christ's death and resurrection, there were churches (i.e. groups of people who sensed this divine calling and responded to it) all over the ancient Near East. John could address the last book of the Bible to seven such churches along an ancient route in present-day Turkey. So, let's keep this in mind: whatever meanings the word 'church' has acquired, it has, first of all, to do with people!

This insight is vital when we ask ourselves how important it is to belong to a church. One of the most famous and most repeated statements from the medieval Catholic Church, codified in 1215 during an important church meeting (Second Lateran Council), was *Extra Ecclesiam Nulla Salus.* This Latin phrase declares: Outside of the Church there is no Salvation. Few believers – and that would also apply to many contemporary Roman Catholics – would agree with the implication of this statement that no one can be accepted by God unless she becomes a baptized member of the Roman Catholic Church. There is no biblical basis for this type of assertion with regard to any church organization. Although I have made a very conscious choice to be a member of a particular denomination (the Seventh-day Adventist Church, which I believe, is closest to the Bible in what it teaches), I will always strongly disagree with any fellow-believer who claims that the only route to eternity is through the door of an Adventist church.

In a different sense, however, this classical statement about the role of the church in our salvation is not so far off the mark. Belonging to the church – to be part of the people of God – is a crucial part of our spiritual journey and not just one option for our spiritual nurture among many. We may find it difficult to see the exact demarcations between the 'church' and the 'world' in the sense that *we* often cannot tell whether a person is indeed part of the people of God. That is, however, not of primary importance. As long as *God* knows who belongs to him, there is no problem. We may also at times wonder whether the church is 'good' enough to qualify as the people of God. The answer is that we will have to be content with the paradox that the church is a community – and, by extension, a sisterhood of such communities – of 'saints' (people who have made a conscious choice and are 'separate'), while, at the same time, it remains a school for sinners! If in doubt about the fact that there are *sinners* in the church, who are nonetheless addressed as *saints*, read the description of Paul of some of the church members in the Greek city of Corinth.[136]

The fact that the Jesus movement was so quickly transformed into the Christian church was not an accident of history. Many historical events do indeed result from a set of unpremeditated circumstances, when someone happened to be somewhere or happened to say or do something at precisely the right or the wrong moment. But that is not how the church originated. Neither was it the fruit of careful strategic planning by apostles like Peter and Paul, nor by later popes, or by church leaders like Martin Luther, John Calvin, Charles Wesley, Menno Simons or Ellen G. White. The church is the church of Jesus Christ because he initiated it. When, almost at the end of the period of Jesus' earthly life, Peter confessed his faith in his Master, Jesus responded by declaring that this faith in him was to be the foundation on which *he* would build his church! [137]

If Christ wanted a church, who are we to argue whether or not it is important to be part of the church – to belong to the people of God? Christ wanted the church as *his people*, that is what matters. Whether we want to belong to God's people or not, God wants a people, he has a people, and he will save this people. (The question is: Can we do without it?) The apostles became the nucleus of the leadership of the people of God. Not because they were naturally endowed with exceptional leadership skills, but because they were 'called out' and were supernaturally enabled to get *his* (not *their*) church going.

In reading about the church's earliest history (in the book of Acts and in the letters the apostles wrote to first-century local communities of Christians) as well as in other early Christian documents which were not included in the Bible, we find that, from its inception, the church was concerned about its efficiency. From the very start the church considered itself an organization. It did not take long before the members in the various local communities appointed leaders. They elected men (and possibly also women[138]) as deacons and elders and other leaders. They agreed on job descriptions, and the apostles provided them with some guidelines as to the criteria that applied to candidates for local leadership. From time to time representatives of the churches met to discuss mutual concerns. Acts chapter fifteen is the earliest record of such a 'council'.

But in its descriptions of the church, the biblical focus is not primarily on any organizational chart (or *organogram* as these things are now called); the Bible does not report that the church adopted a constitution with a respectable series of by-laws, and it would be pushing things to claim that the New Testament provides us with an embryonic Church Manual. The authors of the New Testament pay much more attention to the *nature* of the church. It is not one organization among many, but it is unique. As so often, also in this instance, the Bible uses symbols or metaphors to express a truth that everyday human words cannot communicate. The first such symbol is that of a *woman*. This has nothing to do with the unfortunate reality that men tend to be less inclined to attend church or to become church members than women. There is a totally different kind of message. The *female-male* and *wedding* imagery points to the intimate relationship between Jesus Christ and his church. Repeatedly, Christ is referred to as the Groom, who anxiously waits for his bride (the church), ready for the heavenly wedding. What symbolism could be found that expresses a greater closeness and intimacy?[139] Linked to this metaphor of the 'bride', the followers of Christ are also depicted in a collective way as a woman.[140] This particular woman who symbolizes all the people of God, is 'clothed with the sun', while all those who refuse to identify with the people of God are likewise referred to as a 'woman'. But the woman who symbolizes rejection of, and rebellion against, God is dressed in 'purple' and her further description leaves little to the imagination.[141]

A second, also very powerful, symbol for the church is that of the human *body*. Christ, we are told, is the head and we are all members of that one body – each of us with a special function.[142] The body is a conglomerate of organs. All are important and all are needed if the body is to be healthy, fully functional, fertile and productive. If some organs cease to function, the entire organism falls into disarray, and invalidity, or even death, will result. Some members of the church may have an inflated sense of their worth, and it is easy to consider some prominent or extra-gifted members as more important than the elderly ladies and some recently arrived immigrant members who sit in the back of the church auditorium. But that is not the way God looks at his body. Earlier in life, when I was (I am told) somewhat of a workaholic, I was at times worried that I might suffer a heart attack if I continued in the way I operated. After having lost a gallbladder, and after a treatment for prostate cancer and experiencing a few other medical scares, I am now painfully aware of the fact that my body has lots of other organs that are just as essential as my heart. It has taught me a lesson or two about the powerful image of the church as a body!

The body metaphor tells us that we should not regret that church members differ from one another in many ways, because this is precisely God's explicit intention. All have their own role to play, according to the gifts they possess.[143] There is a place for professionals. There is a need for people who provide leadership and to whom proper respect is due. But in spite of such functional distinctions – and that is the unique but glorious difference between the church and any other organization – all members have exactly the same status. No exception! Theologians refer to this aspect as 'the priesthood of all believers'. Some people may tell you that the church needs a hierarchy of clergy, who are superior to the non-clergy. They are totally, absolutely, two hundred per cent wrong! There is no such difference in status. The prayer of the pope, of Billy Graham, or of the president of my church has no greater value than my prayer and that of any member in the church. We all share the same fundamental status before God! All believers are in a certain sense 'ministers', who as 'priests' serve as a communication medium, doing all they can to bring unbelievers into contact with the God who made them. Together, we pool all our talents and gifts, energies and resources, to live as Christ's body in the world.[144]

Rituals

When we are not fully acquainted with their meaning, rituals may strike us as odd or unappealing. At times we find it difficult to distinguish between traditional folklore and religious rites. All churches have certain rituals, though in some religious communities they tend to be more prominent and elaborate than in others. Some of that depends on theology, but a lot also on culture and tradition. It is clear, however, that people seem to need rituals when they are at important junctions in their own lives, or when extraordinary things happen around them. Interestingly enough, we see how many new rituals emerge wherever religious rituals have been abandoned. This is particularly apparent when a popular idol dies. The unexpected worldwide commotion (some would say hysteria) when Princess Diana died is a poignant reminder of this fact. The gullibility and the willingness of people to submit to often bizarre rites in their worship of nature, or as they experiment with magic, Wicca or even Satanism, is likewise astounding. But even the more mundane rituals – the lighting of a candle in a church, blowing out the candles on our birthday cake, taking our spouse out for dinner on our wedding anniversary or bringing flowers before the start of the weekend – are so firmly established that they will most likely be with us for a long time. (That is how we are made – we need rituals. Just think of all the rituals which God so thoughtfully provided for his people in Old Testament times.)

The church needs rituals because people continue to need them. They transmit important non-verbal messages which are just as important as the verbal communications which come through Bible reading, congregational singing and preaching. Ordination rituals which mark the moment when a pastor, or an elder or deacon, is formally charged with a particular assignment, somehow communicate to those who are ordained, as well as to those who witness the event, that the assignment is more than a job or a next step in a career. It is more than a formal announcement that so-and-so is now such-and-such. It somehow conveys in a powerful manner that God has a hand in what is happening and that he has, in fact, made the appointment and is ready to equip the person for his task.

The two most impressive and important rituals are, no doubt, baptism and the communion service. Baptism marks the entry of a believer into the church. After a public declaration of their faith, new believers are immersed in water. It is a powerful symbol of the 'death' and 'burial' of their former approach to life and of their 'resurrection' towards a new mode of being. It also signifies a kind of spiritual cleansing.[145] It is not some kind of magic that suddenly transforms the one who is baptized into a faultless being. But, just as a marriage ceremony puts its seal on a decision to belong to someone and be faithful to that person, the rite of baptism seals the decision to belong to Christ and his church, and to be faithful to the principles of the faith. This is what Jesus Christ modelled to us when he was baptized,[146] and what complies with the instructions he left to his disciples just prior to his departure from this world.[147]

Those who have travelled in the Near East and have visited the ruins of church buildings dating from the early centuries of the Christian era will have noticed that these buildings always had a baptistery in which people could be immersed. There are, in addition, numerous ancient pictures which illustrate this mode of baptism. As time went by, many denominations replaced this original form of baptism with the sprinkling of infants – in total disregard of the biblical meaning of baptism. The original Greek word *baptizein* literally means 'to immerse', suggesting that plenty of water is needed for baptism.[148] Baptism by immersion continues to be practised by Baptists, Pentecostals, Adventists, and many others.

Another important Christian ritual is that of the Lord's Supper or, as it is also often called, the Communion Service (while some Christian traditions use the term Eucharist). Just before Christ was arrested and executed, he instructed his disciples to remember his passion on a regular basis through a solemn rite. He broke some bread, blessed it and shared that with his disciples, and told them that this broken bread symbolized his 'broken' body. By eating a small piece of this bread the disciples identified with their Lord and were reminded that Christ's death was for them. Then they drank some wine from the cup which Jesus had blessed, in remembrance of the blood that Jesus was to shed on their behalf and on that of all mankind. This rite, they were told, was to be repeated regularly by the Christ-believers right up to the time when Jesus would come a second time.[149] Because the Bible nowhere specifies how often this special service was to take place, different practices have arisen, but in some form or another this ritual has been preserved in almost every Christian community. In some churches it is preceded by another meaningful symbol – foot washing – which even today proves to be a dramatic lesson in strengthening, or restoring, interpersonal relationships.[150]

Symbols speak a language of their own. When children see the golden M, they immediately have a vision of Ronald the clown and of 'happy meals'. When we see the yellow shell we know we have found a place where we can fill our petrol tank. When I drive behind a car with the emblem of a stylized fish on its rear window I know its driver is a person who wants me to know that she is a Christian. The picture of two people exchanging rings never fails to communicate a message of love and mutual commitment. In most cultures the sharing of a meal means far more than just a servicing of our physical needs. It has overtones of warmth, welcome and friendship. In a similar way, participating in the communion service is an experience which cannot be 'deconstructed' into a simple act of eating a morsel of bread and taking a sip from a small cup. It impacts the participant far more than any sermon ever will. Those who 'eat and drink' experience the unique inner assurance that their sins are forgiven and that they are accepted by their God.

But do we really need to join?

Yet I realize that many will find it problematic actually to join a church. Does becoming a member of an organization not restrict our freedom? And does the church, in fact, have the kind of track record that encourages us to join? Moreover, if you are looking for a church to join, how do you choose the right one? These are valid questions.

It cannot be denied that the church has a dark side. A quick scan of the church's history produces a long list of events which flagrantly contradict the example of the One who founded the church. In his name the meanest and most degrading practices have been condoned or at times even promoted. Too often for comfort, church leaders have been greedy for power and money, and have focused on their own status and authority rather than on serving their Lord in all due humility. And this is not just something of a distant past. There are plenty of incidents in contemporary Christianity that tell a sordid tale of unchristian motivations and machinations on the part of those who are supposed to serve the world with honesty and integrity. The scandals that have plagued various television ministries and the abuse of young people by clergymen, and many other deplorable situations, readily spring to mind. Let me be clear: There is no excuse whatsoever for such things!

But, fortunately, it is only a part of the full picture. Even though there is no perfect community of believers, there are many places where people have found a safe spiritual roof over their heads – a place where they feel welcome and where they 'belong'; where they feel supported and nurtured. Personally I have met so many Christian men and women who professed, lived and shared their faith in such a marvellous way that I have often felt humbled and left in awe. I have read widely in the annals of church history and I have often been profoundly impressed by the tales of heroic martyrdom and of unremitting dedication in the face of great hardships. I have worked with colleagues whom I continue to admire for their devotion, discipline and servant-leadership.

Few statements about this paradoxical reality of the church – about its dark and its light side – are so to the point as the words of Ellen G. White, a nineteenth-century woman who left a literary legacy of tens of thousands of pages. She wrote that 'the church of Christ, enfeebled and defective as it may be, is the only object on earth on which he bestows his supreme regard.'[151] God worked in the days of old with less than perfect people. Christ picked less than perfect people as the core group for the new movement that was to emerge. And it is no different today. The church is, and remains, God's church in spite of all human inconsistencies and failings. 'The church is what it is because of who Jesus is, not because of who its members are.'[152]

Joining a church is important for our spiritual life. It is good for us and for our inner life to meet regularly with others who have similar aims and ideals and struggle with similar questions and problems.[153] It is the place where the right side of our brain is enriched by the rituals we described above and by the beauty of language, architecture and music; and where the left side of our brain is engaged in acquiring a deeper understanding of the faith and its implications for our daily lives. It is a place where gender and race, age and profession lose their divisive tendencies, because we know we are all brothers and sisters – children of the same heavenly Father, with Christ as our 'elder brother'.[154]

One thing must, however, be constantly kept in mind: the church is all about participation. Remember the image of the body? Not just participation through our bodily presence and our financial contributions. *Being part of the church is being part of the mission of the church!* Brian McLaren writes in his fascinating book about 'a new kind of Christian',

'In my thinking, the church does not exist for the benefit of its members. It exists to equip its members for the benefit of the world. To do that, it is about three things: community, spirituality and mission.

'Community means that we create a place of belonging where people can learn to believe the good news, belonging to a community that is learning to behave (or live) by it, and become (together) a living example of it.'[155]

Michael Riddell underlines that church members cannot be passive consumers, who pick and choose the elements they like, and enjoy coming along for the ride. A church which has mostly that kind of members will not survive. He says, 'When the church becomes another leisure activity for the comfortable, it does not do well in the face of competition.'[156] The church is more than a club of likeminded people. It is infinitely more than spiritual amusement. It is a place where we are equipped for mission.

This may not be the kind of picture of the church that you had expected or that many 'churchy' people seem to have. There is, indeed, quite a contrast between the idea many people have inherited about the church and the biblical model. (1) The Bible characterizes the church as a living organism rather than primarily an organization. (2) It sees the church in terms of people rather than in terms of programmes. (3) It places spirituality high above authority. (4) The biblical picture of the church is one of service, and not of control. And, (5) it does not primarily concentrate on itself and its own comfort, but on its mission.[157] We will return to this aspect in the final chapter.

Which church?

In the past people tended to choose the denomination their parents and grandparents belonged to, and were inclined to become members of the nearest church community of that denomination. If your parents were Lutheran, it would be 'normal' to join the Lutheran church, preferably in the town where you happen to live. If your family was Catholic, chances were that you would also become and remain a Catholic.

This pattern is now much less common than it was only a generation ago. Many people who have come to the decision that they want to join a church take their time to shop for the congregation that suits their personal preferences and their family situation. Who is the pastor? Is he a good preacher? Are there enough activities for our children? Does the music fit my taste? How far is the church from where I live? Is it easy to park? How 'open' is the church for newcomers?

These, and many other questions, are legitimate. But they should not be the only, or even the most important ones, in our search for a church. The most important question will always have to be: How faithful is a church to the teachings of the Bible? That is not to say that it does not matter how the members of a church behave, or how they relate to visitors, as long as they try to be faithful to biblical doctrine. What a church stands for must not only be heard but also be seen. Whether or not a church attempts to stay close to the principles of the Bible should be uppermost in our minds when we choose a church. That is the reason why I have chosen to be a Seventh-day Adventist Christian. Not because it is the most perfect church in terms of how church members act and relate to each others. I see in my church things I do not like, even though the vast majority of my fellow believers are fine people who truly live their faith. In the final analysis, I have become an Adventist and stayed an Adventist, because I believe I have found a church that is committed to the message of the Bible – and not just in a theoretical way. It is a church that is interested in the *head* and the *heart*, but also in what our *hands* can do in the praxis of life. And, above all, it is strongly mission-driven! Although it wants to remain faithful to what God revealed many centuries ago, it is a church that is in tune with the times.

I fully agree with Lee Strobel when he said, 'If Christianity requires a person to become a societal misfit who has no social life except church services and prayer meetings, count me out.'[158] I want to live in the twenty-first century and try to speak the language of the twenty-first century, and do my best to understand the thinking of the twenty-first century, while remaining faithful to the values of a first-century Person.

Deciding to be a Christian, and carefully choosing a community where you want to be a member is quite a step. But countless men and women have testified that becoming involved with a church family was the best decision they ever made. They have found that in joining a church,

'. . . we connect ourselves not only to the God who created and brought people together in the first place, but to all those past, present, and future who seek to know God and live in faith every day. . . . Attempting to live in isolation or to make our spirituality a private affair rejects a part of our nature and goes against the very manner of living that God intends for us. Going to church then connects us with God, each other, and the world.'[159]

I end this chapter with a statement made by C. S. Lewis, one of the greatest Christian authors of the last century: 'If you are thinking of becoming a Christian, I warn you that you are embarking on something that is going to take the whole out of you, brains and all.'[160] He is totally right. Becoming a Christian does not only take your brains. It takes all of you, as we shall see in the next chapter.

Chapter eight

Responsibility

Today's Dutch society is one of the most secular in the world. Yet only a few decades ago life in the Low Countries was strictly organized along confessional lines: Protestant, Catholic or 'neutral'. The farmers were organized into a Protestant farmers' union, a Roman Catholic farmers' union and a non-religious farmers' union. The same pattern applied to shopkeepers, civil servants, employers, and . . . you name it. The right to broadcast radio and television programmes was distributed among a number of broadcasting corporations, which had either a Liberal Protestant, a Conservative Protestant, an Evangelical, a Catholic, a Socialist or a Social-Democrat, etc., charter. The law made provision for Catholic schools, Protestant schools of various persuasions and public schools.

Very little is now left of those traditional structures, as Dutch society has changed possibly even more rapidly and radically than the rest of the Western world. But I continue to wonder why people once thought that all those confessional divisions and subdivisions were needed. For instance, how could the work and the professional interests of a Catholic farmer possibly differ from those of a Protestant farmer? Was there a Catholic way of growing wheat and a Protestant method for increasing milk production? There were actually separate Catholic and Protestant organizations to represent the interests of goat breeders! The deeper reason for this still escapes me. I find it easier to see how 'Christian' labour unions differed from their non-Christian counterparts, for instance in the tactics they would use in fighting a labour conflict. And I can still see many good reasons why there should be Christian (and Muslim) schools of various kinds and public schools. Yet, in today's secular context, even in the education sector, questions are raised increasingly as to whether or not the proliferation in the domain of education, mainly along religious lines, is productive. Is there a Christian approach to geometry, or a Muslim way of studying French? Is there a Catholic view of geography or a Protestant philosophy of chemistry?

Even though I will not defend many of the elements of the traditional system I knew in my childhood days, I nevertheless feel that there is nowadays an unfortunate tendency to de-link completely what we *do* from what we *believe*. It may be true that our beliefs hardly impact on the way in which we study algebra and geography or breed goats. But our religious convictions do interface in many ways with areas as biology and history, and with the way in which we do business. And our religious or non-religious persuasion may direct us in the choice of the books we want to read as we master a language! And so on.

I see it as one of the unfortunate aspects of postmodernity that people increasingly live fragmented lives. The norms and values which govern one particular aspect of their existence are frequently not synchronized with those which are operational in other areas of their lives. According to the postmodern view man lives his life in different compartments, on different 'floors' of his house, and what he does on one 'floor' often has very little to do with what he is and does on another 'floor.' The Christian will, however, take issue with that idea. The Christian faith does not operate on one 'floor' only, but pervades the entire 'house'. It has as much to do with what we *do* as with what we *believe*. It is a way of life. Jesus once said, If you believe in me and follow me, 'you will know the truth, and the truth will set you free.'[161] In other words: When you have the 'truth', it not only informs you about what is theoretically true, but it also *does* something for you. It impacts on your actions and on all aspects of your life. You find this same concept echoed when you turn the page where the text I just referred to is found. There Jesus is quoted as saying, 'I have come that people may *have life*, and *have it to the full!*'[162]

Two key words stand out as we search the Bible for clues about this full, abundant life that is on offer: *discipleship* and *stewardship*. The word 'disciple' is derived from the Latin *discipulus*, which means pupil or adherent. Disciples are people who follow a 'master'. They are willing to be instructed by him, they want to be around him and assist him, and are eager to adopt his philosophy and life style as their own. Stewards are people who are entrusted with certain responsibilities; they are given the responsibility of looking after particular interests as if these were their own. But they do not forget that they are not the owner; they have been charged with ensuring the maximum profit for their master, and can expect to be properly rewarded if they prove to be diligent and trustworthy. It requires a clear choice and a solid determination to be a disciple of Christ.[163] The Master himself said, 'If you hold to my teachings, you are really my disciples.'[164]

The concepts of discipleship and stewardship are closely related. One cannot be a good disciple without being a faithful steward. This chapter will focus on what it means to be a steward. Jesus told a few stories (parables) to explain the fundamental concept. One of these is found in Matthew chapter 25, where he refers to a man who went on a long journey and entrusted his property to his servants. One received five 'talents', another two, and yet another only one. Two of those stewards did well. Each was able to show a hundred per cent profit upon the master's return. But one just sat on what he had received, and did nothing with it. This steward was punished severely. A similar story is recorded in the gospel of Luke. The *dramatis personae* and the numbers are different, but the moral of the story is the same.[165]

Caretakers of God's creation

Stewardship has to do with everything we have received in trust and what we do with it: our life, our time, our health, our skills and our material resources. But let's begin with the larger picture. I return to an aspect which I have already emphasized several times: We owe our existence to our Creator, the Designer-God, who made us and continues to be deeply interested in us. We are part of his creation and have been given an important role in caring for it. At the very beginning man was told that he was to look after the earth. He was supposed to 'subdue' the earth and 'rule' (or, as another translation puts it: be the 'master'[166]) over all non-human living creatures.[167] This was part of God's blessing for his highest creature. Men and women were charged to be fruitful and to fill the earth. Man was to be God's appointed agent in keeping his creation in order. The very first thing man was told to do was to give a name to all the different 'living creatures'.[168] The first couple was placed in ideal surroundings – Paradise, or the Garden of Eden – and they were to tend it and 'take care' of it.[169]

Looking back on the history of mankind we must acknowledge that the human race has performed rather poorly, in particular in the last two hundred years, in which we have moved from utilising the resources of this planet to a ruthless exploitation of them and to large scale destruction of the human habitat. 'Subduing' the earth has turned into 'exploiting' it; 'ruling' has become 'lording over', and 'use' has degenerated into 'abuse'.[170] The stewards of this world have become thieves, usurpers and destroyers. This is a very serious matter indeed. It is not mere negligence, but it is disobedience to the divine instructions. It is sin.[171]

Seán McDonagh, a Christian anthropologist, puts it every succinctly. He says, 'Reflection on God's care for and sovereignty over creation reminds Christians that our ethical behaviour is not confined to actions that affects other human beings, but that a violation of creation is also a sin.'[172]

Postmodern people are fully in tune with the biblical view of man's stewardship over the earth. It has become crystal clear to them that the 'modern' greedy exploitation of the resources of this earth will ultimately bring disaster and death. A large percentage of the tropical forests have disappeared. Most of the profits have hardly benefited the people who live in the countries where these forests are found, but have lined the pockets of corrupt politicians in the developing world and Western businessmen. The fossil fuels are being burned up with reckless speed. This has had a major impact on the earth's ecosystems, through severe pollution and, more recently, climate change. In the past three decades, the widespread saturation of ecosystems with nitrogen compounds, such as ammonia and nitrogen oxides from agricultural fertilizers and air pollution, has emerged as an additional global threat. The increase of carbon dioxide and a number of other gases in the atmosphere – commonly referred to as the 'greenhouse effect' – results in a global warming. As the surface of the earth becomes warmer, the ice caps at the poles will be reduced and sea levels will rise. This will have a devastating effect on many Pacific islands, and on countries like Bangladesh. (It also poses a threat to my country, the Netherlands, which is partly below sea level; if the North Sea rises the dikes will have to be drastically reinforced.) Depletion of the ozone layers will increase detrimental solar radiation and will harm both animals and human beings. The 'advanced' nations produce enormous amounts of, often hazardous, waste. In the United Kingdom alone, for example, more than 500 million tons of waste are generated each year. Thousands of species of plant and animal life have disappeared and countless others are seriously endangered. Acid rain is yet another problem. Many seas and lakes are now virtually without fish. In many places the water that is needed to support human and animal life has been polluted by chemical plants and other industries. And the sad story continues almost *ad infinitum*.

Is it too late to turn the tide? Opinions differ. In any case, sweeping changes are needed – now! We may need scores of Kyoto-treaties, with all industrial countries participating, and a revolutionary shift in the distribution of wealth between the developed and the developing world. Those who believe (as I do) in the nearness of the Second Coming of Christ will wonder whether mankind actually has enough time left – even if it were to have the political will and senses the ethical imperative – to undo much of the ecological havoc that has already been wrought. However, though I believe the soon return of Christ is a certainty, and though I am convinced we must count on divine intervention for the ultimate and final restoration of the earth, I see no excuse for leaning back and just letting events run their awful course. If there is one thing clear, it is that we are called to be God's stewards until the very last moment of earth's history. This demands our active involvement and means that we must do all we can do to reverse current trends.

Even though Robert Wuthnow, a prominent Princeton sociologist, is unfortunately right when he observes that 'most churchgoers deplore the greed they see in others, but remain insensitive to its impulses in themselves', we must make sure this cannot be said of us.[173] Those who want to take the mandate to 'care' for the earth seriously, will use all the influence they have to make their society more just and equitable and less wasteful, even if only incremental changes seem possible. As they cast their votes in local and national elections, they will not only think of the economy of their own country, but will consider how everyone's lifestyle, use of the earth's resources, and policies with regard to the developing world, affect the future of this planet and the quality of billions of lives in the poorer areas of this world. We can expect changes on the macro-level only if there are individuals who truly believe that we must be stewards of this earth. Even if the great majority of people would not be willing to change their selfish pattern of consumption and prefer to ignore the alarming messages of environmental experts, this would not change one iota of the mandate for me as an individual – as a created being who has been given a responsibility in 'caring' for God's creation – to be a steward of the beauties and resources of this world.

But what can I do as an individual? Whatever I do will be an infinitesimal drop in the ecological bucket. Nonetheless, I must do what I can. However small is the contribution that I can make, it will serve as a signal to others around me that I want to be a steward of the goods that my Creator has entrusted to me, and it may inspire others to become such stewards also. In final analysis, it is a statement of faith – religion translated not just into words, but into action. And, as we know, actions usually speak considerably louder than words.

What we can and should do depends to a large extent on our personal situation. It is our individual responsibility to determine what we can contribute to the 'saving' of our world. I am painfully aware that I must learn to do better in many areas of my daily life. I have benefited from a booklet I picked up a few years ago which in its simplicity and practicality made eminent sense to me. It lists fifty 'simple things' most of us can do to protect our environment and 'save' our planet. The publication reminds us of the startling fact that the junk mail Americans receive in one day could produce enough energy to heat a quarter of a million homes.[174] In our home, my wife has taken steps to reduce greatly the avalanche of junk-mail and advertising brochures we receive. We make a conscious effort to use fewer plastic bags. We try to save on energy and water, and not just for financial reasons. We try to reduce our household waste and recycle paper, milk cartons, bottles and batteries. We try not to buy things which are unfriendly to the environment. We believe we can make a difference even through small adaptations in the way we live and work. It is part of being stewards of what God has given us.

Stewards of our body

In many countries the issue of whether or not an individual has the right to determine what he does with his own body is still hotly debated. It is at the centre of the legal battles around abortion and euthanasia. In the thinking of many, the crucial question is whether the society or the individual has the last word if a woman wishes to terminate a pregnancy or when she decides that she wants to die. This is an important facet, but there is another, even more fundamental issue: Are we the owners of our body or has our body been entrusted to us by our Creator? If so, he has the final word as to how we treat our bodies, and we must prove to be faithful stewards also of this aspect of our existence.

It is often suggested that religion has to do with the 'soul', with our inner life rather than with the physical aspects of our being. This attitude was quite understandable in a time when there was – in any case among Christians – a widespread belief that the human being consists of a non-material, spiritual component and of a totally separate material, physical, part. As we noted earlier, the postmodern view of man is holistic – spirit and body cannot be separated. This, many Christians now realize, is actually much closer to the biblical view than the traditional theology many churches have held until recently. Our faith in God impacts very definitely on the way we look after our health and the things we eat. Ellen G. White, a well-known nineteenth century Adventist author who wrote on a wide range of topics, was far ahead of her times when she penned these words: 'There is more religion in a loaf of good bread than many of you think. There is more religion in good cooking than you have any idea of.'[175] Many more recent experts likewise stress that physical and spiritual welfare are closely linked. Health, therefore, is more than the absence of physical problems. This is underlined by Leo R. van Dolson and J. Robert Spangler in their book *Healthy, Happy, Holy*: 'The body is to be under the control of a regenerated mind. . . . The truly healthy person, from the biblical viewpoint, is one who is physically well, mentally alert, socially concerned, and spiritually committed.'[176]

There are numerous indications in the Bible that God is interested in our bodies and in the way we treat them. Paul encourages the Christians not just to put their mind and spirit in tune with the divine Spirit, but also to offer their *bodies* as a sacrifice to God. Obviously, he is not referring to any bizarre ritual of human sacrifice, but wants his readers to realize that they are responsible for the use and upkeep of their bodies. This concept is even more clearly expressed in his letter to the Corinthian Christians:

'Do you not know that your body is a temple of the Holy Spirit, who is in you, whom you have received from God? You are not your own; you were bought at a price. Therefore honour God with your body.'[177]

It stands to reason that we should try to keep our bodies in good working (and running) order. Health is not just a general *human* concern, it is also, in a very special way, a *Christian* concern. It was very clearly a concern of Christ. He did not care only for people's spiritual needs by addressing their feelings of sin and guilt, but he also met their physical needs as he healed many of the sick he encountered, and on a few occasions he even arranged for them to be fed.

Under inspiration, Moses provided the people of Israel with some specific guidelines regarding personal hygiene and sanitation, and with a detailed list of animal produce that was considered unfit for human consumption.[178] Practising these rules would go a long way to controlling and containing communicable diseases and to guaranteeing a decent level of sanitation. 'Obedience to the moral code of the Ten Commandments and paying attention to the various regulations about cleanliness was an important factor in avoiding sexually-transmitted diseases. The dietary laws clearly decreased the intake of saturated fats and cholesterol.'[179] Adherence to these stipulations, which include (among other things) the abstinence from pork and seafood, resulted in greater health and a longer life.[180] Van Dolson and Spangler insist that although these sanitary and dietary laws in the Old Testament do not have the same status as the Law of the Ten Commandments they can only be discarded to our detriment:

'[We should not] suggest that all Hebrew laws and regulations have been shown scientifically correct or sensible by current popular understanding, but many writers are impressed that their laws and restrictions resulted in healthier and more sanitary conditions. We cannot escape the conclusion that an all-wise God did intend that conformity to these laws would result in healthier, happier, and holier people.'[181]

There is plenty of scientific evidence that lifestyle has a lot to do with life expectancy. In the last few decades some 250 studies on Seventh-day Adventists have been conducted in the United States, but also in Europe and Central America. Though the figures vary, they show without exception that Adventists live on average several years longer than the general population. In some countries Adventist men live almost ten years longer than the average male population. For women the difference is a bit smaller but still remarkable.[182]

What are the reasons why Seventh-day Adventists, on average, live so much longer than most people around them?[183] Several studies have shown that faith has a positive influence on a person's health. But there are also a number of important lifestyle principles at work. Adventists do not smoke and say 'no' to alcohol. If they eat meat – many are vegetarians – they tend to eat it in small quantities and of the leaner varieties, while avoiding the animal products which ancient Israel was told not to use for consumption. No doubt many Adventists would live even longer than they already do if they would not only follow these principles, but would also be more serious about some other aspects of healthful living, such as avoiding stress; maintaining a careful balance between work and free time; and, in particular, taking enough physical exercise and maintaining their ideal weight. Surely, if we truly believe that our body is a 'temple' of God's Spirit, we will try to keep it clean and in a good state of repair. It is hard to understand why people intentionally harm it by the use of tobacco and other harmful substances. And the tradition of abstinence from alcoholic beverages definitely fits in with this stewardship concept regarding our health. Our bodies are intricate parts of God's creation and are 'wonderfully made.'[184] As his stewards we are therefore expected to keep our bodies in optimum condition.

Being good stewards of our bodies does not mean that we should aspire to the ascetic ideal, or that our lives must become totally focused on what we eat or drink, or, especially, on what we should *not* eat and *not* drink. After all, life is more than food, as Jesus himself declared.[185] And Christ was not averse to a good party with a rich buffet.[186] His followers should feel free to enjoy life, and eating and drinking are part of the enjoyment of life. But while they enjoy themselves, they will always remember that their bodies are not their own, and therefore they will do what they can to keep them in good condition, inwardly and outwardly. Not because this happens to be trendy, or because it is good for their public image, but because it is something they will gladly do to honour the One who calls himself their Master.

Christian time management

Do Christians manage their time better than non-Christians? Some recent studies indicate that 'conservative' Christians work harder and longer than the average person. Just over a century ago a classic study by the famous German economist and sociologist Max Weber (1864-1920) defended the thesis that certain elements in the Calvinistic version of Protestantism have encouraged a work ethic that stimulated the development of Western capitalism.[187] If true, not everybody will consider this as a one hundred per cent positive contribution.

Whether or not Weber was right is still a topic for debate. And whether Christians today are really better in their management of time than people in general is difficult to determine. If there are any current scientific studies on this topic, I have not seen them. However, it must be stated that there *should* be a marked difference. Christian stewardship will influence us in our use of time. The way Christians manage their time should be anchored in the weekly day of rest on the seventh day. The rhythm of six 'normal' days, followed by a period of twenty-four 'holy' hours, provides us with the basic pattern for our activities. But the fact that one in seven days is set apart for a special use, does not mean that religion has nothing to do with the other six. Some things are not appropriate on the seventh day, but there are also quite a few things which are inappropriate on any day of the week. Many people claim that you should try to experience whatever is within your reach. You only live once, they say. If there are things you have never tried you may have missed out on some good fun or some exciting adventure. People who reason this way seem to think that any kind of activity will enrich their life. The Christian view, however, is that not all activities carry a plus sign. There are also activities which are accompanied by a minus sign. They do not add to the abundant life that Christ promises, but rather obstruct the abundant life that can be ours. True enough, you only live once. So, don't waste part of your life.

The sad truth is that most of us waste enormous amounts of time. Some of us suffer from a chronic lack of personal organization; many of us refuse to read the owner's manual when we purchase a new piece of equipment and will lose precious hours while trying to solve sudden problems by a time-consuming tactic of trial and error. We can waste a lot of time by reading pulp magazines or novels, or viewing soaps which have neither interesting content nor artistic quality. Many – in particular men – regularly waste a significant amount of time because of their reluctance to admit their limitations and ask questions or seek assistance. Obviously, wasting time is at variance with good time management. On the other hand, there is no suggestion in the Bible that we should make every minute useful and productive, and can never sit back and simply relax and enjoy ourselves. Again, Jesus is our role model. Even a cursory reading of the gospels will show that Jesus was no workaholic. He was a people person, who had time for his friends, enjoyed a good meal and regularly took time 'off'. The key to proper time management is balance. Read what a wise man some three thousand years ago had to say. A few of these lines may sound somewhat strange to us, but the overall message is clear:

> 'There is a time for everything and a season
> for every activity under heaven:
> a time to be born and a time to die,
> a time to plant and a time to uproot,
> a time to kill and a time to heal,
> a time to tear down and a time to build,
> a time to weep and a time to laugh,
> a time to mourn and a time to dance,
> a time to scatter stones and a time to gather them,
> a time to embrace and a time to refrain,
> a time to search and a time to give up,
> a time to keep and a time to throw away,
> a time to tear and a time to mend,
> a time to be silent and a time to speak,
> a time to love and a time to hate,
> a time for war and a time for peace.
>
> God will bring to judgment both the righteous
> and the wicked,
> For there will be a time for every activity, a time
> for every deed.'[188]

There is a time for all kinds of different activities. A time for work and for hobbies; a time for play and a time for concentrated work; a time for voluntary work and a time for the family; a time to go for a solitary walk and a time to socialize; a time to meditate and a time to party; a time to read a good book; and a time to wash the car; a time to worship and a time to take the children to Disneyworld. There must be a healthy balance. Spending all our time on our knees is just as imbalanced as spending all our time watching soccer. And using every free minute to surf the Internet shows the same lack of balance as using every night of the week in church-related voluntary work.

Of course, there is always more to do than we have time for. We must therefore constantly prioritize. And so – while all we said in the previous paragraph is true – God has first call on us as we seek to manage our time. And our spouse and family come a very close second, with our friends not far behind. Relationships have top priority in the 'full' life that can be ours. Good stewards will not only be intentional in the way they spend their time in their professional life, but will be generous in giving time to the people that matter to them most.

A philosophy of sharing

Being a steward has, as we saw, to do with concern for the earth, and also with care for our body and the use of our time. In addition, it has to do with the skills and talents we possess. Just think of the way we can use our creativity. We can enlist our creative abilities in our pursuit of beauty and ideals, but they can also be used in vulgar and debasing projects. How we direct our creative juices is a direct outflow of the fundamental choice we are urged to make. As disciples of the Lord, we will see our abilities and creative talents as gifts we are privileged to use in the service of the Master and to the benefit of other people. Stewardship of our talents, however, goes further. Most of us have more skills and abilities than we realize, or fail to develop at least some of them to their full potential. Many of us prefer to use the left side of our brain, while neglecting the right side. If we are in that category, we should remember the admonition of the Lord that we must serve him, not only with all of our 'heart' and all of our 'soul', but also with *all* our 'mind' – right side and left side![189]

Christian stewardship includes the express desire to develop and multiply our talents. Allow me to illustrate how multiplication works. I did not grasp the true scope of the concept of multiplication until I read Mike Nappa's inspiring book *The Courage to*

Be a Christian. He tells the story of a Mr Webster who offered to hire someone for one month. The prospective employee had a choice as to the form of payment. He could opt for one million dollars cash at the end of the month or choose to receive one penny on his first day of work, and then have his wage doubled every day until the end of the month. [I knew that Einstein had once said that the greatest mathematical discovery of all time is compound interest, but it took this story to bring that message home.] I made the calculation what it would mean to start with one penny and then see the amount doubled every day for a full month, and to my utter surprise, I discovered that the total wages for those 30 days would amount to well over 10 million dollars![190]

The multiplication of our talents may not work quite at this rate over such a short period, but we may be in for some real surprises, for the divine arithmetic differs significantly from ours, as we will also see below.

Of course, when discussing 'stewardship', sooner or later we will have to talk about money. When I sit in the pew and listen to a sermon on stewardship I know that before I hear the preacher say 'amen', I will be challenged to be more generous with my wallet or credit card in support of my church. And, sure enough, that is also the direction in which this chapter now moves. I could have started with this aspect, but I hope that by now it has become clear that I do not see stewardship only, or even primarily, in terms of dollars, euros, pounds or yens. Yet stewardship is also about how we handle money. Again there are a few basic principles. God is the owner of everything. What we posses is not our own, but is entrusted in our care, and we are supposed to look after it responsibly and faithfully.

Christian stewardship often seems to be in stark contrast with common sense. The philosophy of our society is that earning and receiving should come before spending. Receiving money is pleasant, while spending money can easily become a rather worrisome experience, especially if one sees that the money is not coming in quickly enough to cover all expenses. We can only become richer when receiving outpaces spending. I am not going to advocate that we can spend without restraint, regardless of what we receive now or expect to receive in the future, but there is definitely a sense in which spending is much more pleasant than receiving. Allow these words of Jesus to sink in for a few moments: *'It is more blessed to give than to receive.'*[191] The apostle Paul underlines this notion further when he says, 'Remember this: Whoever sows sparingly will also reap sparingly, and *whoever sows generously, will also reap generously* ... for God loves a cheerful giver.'[192] Through his prophet Malachi (see the last pages of the Old Testament) God encouraged the people of Israel to be generous in their giving to what was then the equivalent of the church. 'Test me', he said, 'and see if I will not throw open the floodgates of heaven and pour out so much blessing that you will not have enough room for it.'[193]

One of the first questions that tend to arise when people discuss their financial support for the church – the organization that has been delegated in a special way with the preaching of the good news and with the spiritual care for those who have declared their allegiance to Christ and have discovered the significance of belonging to a community of believers – is how much one ought to give for that purpose. Some begin their calculations while secretly harbouring a fear that giving to the church may take too large a bite out of their budget. To them the unspoken question often is not, 'How much is required of me?' or 'How much could I give if I really tried?' but 'How little can I get away with?' This kind of reasoning shows an unfortunate ignorance or disregard for what it is to be a steward of what God has given into our care. Let me just refer to two Bible passages to illustrate this point.

Example number one: Ananias and Sapphira, husband and wife, were members of the church in Jerusalem. It was shortly after the church had been founded and the early enthusiasm was still at a premium height. Several people concluded that giving all their material possessions to the advancement of their newfound ideal was the logical thing to do. Ananias and Sapphira decided they also wanted to show their generosity, so they sold a piece of land and brought most of the proceeds to the church leaders, but they kept back part of the money for themselves. The impression one gets when reading the story is that a major portion of the income from the sale was donated to the church. Instead of lavish praise for this remarkable degree of generosity there was, however, only severe condemnation. In between the lines we read that the primary motive of this couple was their desire to be seen as generous![194]

Example number two: Look at a few lines at the beginning of Luke chapter 21. Jesus saw how some rich people were bringing their gifts to the temple treasury and then noticed how a poor widow also put 'two very small copper coins' into the offering box. He said, 'I tell you the truth, this poor widow put in more than all the others.'[195]

You get the point? The amount we give is not of prime importance but the spirit that motivates our giving. A generous person does not get poorer when she shares her money with others, but stands to be blessed because of her generosity.[196] A person who gives for the wrong reason will receive no blessing at all. But how much do we give? Is there no guideline at all? Yes, there is. The apostle Paul encouraged the church members to be systematic in their giving.[197] That clearly makes sense. If we deal systematically with mortgage payments and car loans, with the savings for our old age, and with the expenses for a lot of other important aspects of daily life, it would be strange if we were not to make our giving also an important part of our budgeting process. If we are looking for further biblical counsel on this topic, we soon discover that systematic giving in Old Testament times took the form of giving a tenth of one's income 'to God' for the running of his affairs. This same principle, it seems, is taken for granted in the New Testament.[198] Whether or not there is hard proof in the New Testament that 'tithing' is still to be viewed as a commandment is, I believe, of little importance. Giving that is based on a sense of being forced to comply with a minimum norm, or that issues from fear, is not the kind of giving that brings a blessing (see example one above). There is another way of looking at it. If ten per cent was the norm in Old Testament times, how could we – who know so much more about what God has done for us than the people of old knew, and who understand the urgency of communicating the good news so much clearer – be less generous than they were? Instead of giving less than a 'tithe', it would be natural to give more! [Of course, although we give 'with a cheerful heart', we must require of those who handle the money that is cheerfully given, to do so with great care and transparency. They must be stewards in a very special sense.]

Rich people and financial prosperity are not condemned in the Bible. That is just as well, for let's face it, the vast majority of those who live in the developed world are 'rich' in comparison with those who live in the slums of Calcutta, in Mexico City or in the villages of sub-Saharan Africa. The constant emphasis in the Bible on the responsibility of the rich for the poor is, therefore, not just a message addressed to Bill Gates or Donald Trump, but one that is also addressed to most of us. Those who have the good fortune to live in the affluent part of the world must be willing to share with those – near and far – who have little or nothing at all. God always sides with the poor, and a relationship with him will automatically result in solidarity with those who, through no fault of their own, live in poverty. While working on this part of the chapter I noticed a recent report of UNICEF, which stated that almost half of all children in the world (approximately 1 billion!) are the victims of war, hunger or disease. How can I not be moved by such statistics and share some of what I have with those children?

Lots of books have been written about the money aspect of stewardship. Some give very good counsel but, in final analysis, we will all have to look at our own situation and must try to determine what good stewardship entails in our particular circumstances. A key word is 'simplicity'. Our lives 'should be marked by voluntary abstinence in the midst of extravagant luxury'. Our use of the resources we have at our disposal should always be tempered by human need.[199] The same author who provided this wise counsel also had this to say:

'Our study of money leads us to the inescapable conclusion: we who follow Jesus Christ are called to a vow of simplicity. This vow is not for the dedicated few but for all. It is not an option to take or leave depending on our personal preference. All who name Christ as Lord and Saviour are obliged to follow what he says, and Jesus' call to discipleship in money can be best summed up in the single word *simplicity*. Simplicity seeks to do justice to our Lord's many-faceted teachings about money – light and dark, giving and receiving, trust, contentment, faith.'[200]

In summary, our religion is not only a matter of intellect and emotion. True religion is translated in how we act and what we do with the things we possess, individually and corporately. Salvation is not earned through any of the stewardship elements we discussed in this chapter. But a Christian who refuses to be a good steward is not a genuine disciple. The apostle James phrased it thus: 'Faith by itself, if it is not accompanied by action, is dead.'[201] Thus it was two thousand years ago and so it is today.

Chapter nine

Commitment

We are approaching the end of our journey of discovery. At the same time, we could also say that we are actually only just getting ready to embark on the adventure of being followers of Jesus Christ. We have discussed the meaning of life. We have talked about the leap of faith that will open up a whole new way of looking at life. We have seen how the Bible plays a unique role in shaping the content of our faith, and we have also looked at some of the practical implications of believing in God. There is, however, one more important aspect that pulls all the threads of our web of 'justifiable beliefs' together (remember chapter two?): full commitment to the One in whom our faith is anchored. In the end, it all boils down to making a clear decision about how we want to live in view of the convictions that give structure to our inner life, and then sticking to this resolve. Speaking about the importance of making the right decisions, Henri Nouwen once said:

'Choices make the difference. Two people are in the same accident and severely wounded. They did not choose to be in the accident. It happened to them. But one of them chose to live the experience in bitterness, the other in gratitude. These choices radically influenced their lives and the lives of their families and friends. We have very little control over what happens in our lives, but we have a lot of control over how we integrate and remember what happens. It is precisely these spiritual choices that determine whether we live our lives with dignity.'[202]

But I realize that postmodern people do not like to make clear-cut choices or irreversible commitments. They have a deep-rooted desire to keep their options open and to stop short of total involvement. They tend to shy away from lifelong careers in one and the same company. They may vote for a particular political party, but hesitate a long time before (if ever) they become fully-fledged members of a political organization. Many will regularly attend a church in which they feel at home, but hesitate to take the final step and ask for baptism and membership. In many developed countries, in particular in Europe, cohabitation has become the rule and marriage is often postponed for many years. Even though a couple may live together and even have children together, they will tell their parents that they are not 'ready' for marriage. For some, often quite irrational, reasons they postpone this final commitment.

Postmodern people apparently hate to burn any bridges that allow for a last-minute escape. However, if the Christian faith truly is what it claims to be, there can be no other valid response than a one hundred per cent 'yes'. There can be no question of a never-ending 'wait and see', of a provisional acceptance or of divided loyalty. Yet for many postmoderns the ultimate decision may come at the end of quite a long process.

The biblical word for the crucial change in our inner orientation, from a state of non-commitment to the God who made and redeemed us to a state of total commitment to him on whom we know we ultimately depend, is *conversion*. This originally Latin word means: a turning around. There must be a point in our lives when that happens. It is a new start, also frequently referred to as a 'new birth.' It is not optional. A Jewish leader once came to Jesus and asked what step he needed to take if he wanted to share in the abundant life – in the here and now and in the hereafter – that Jesus promised. The answer was unequivocal:

Unless you turn around and make a new start – unless you are 'born again' – you will not 'see the kingdom of God', that is: you will remain an outsider and will not truly belong to God's family.[203]

The Bible contains some fascinating conversion stories. Take, for example, the turning around of tax-collector Zacheus. He was even less popular with the citizens of Jerusalem than his present-day colleagues in the Internal Revenue Service are with most of us. For not only did he use all available means to collect the taxes that were due to the authorities, he had also devised a clever scheme which enabled him to enrich himself. But meeting Jesus made the crucial difference in his life, and he 'converted' from a life dedicated to mammon (money) to a career of discipleship.[204] Or, to mention another example – the apostle Paul. At the beginning of the Book of Acts we encounter him as a fanatical opponent of the new Jesus-movement, but one day, while travelling on the road to Damascus with a mission to kill the followers of Jesus Christ in that city, he had a life-changing experience. As a result he turned around and became himself a disciple of the man from Galilee.[205] And there are quite a few other striking biblical examples of such sudden conversions.

We know of many people who, in the course of Christian history, likewise experienced such a sudden turn-around. Martin Luther's story is probably the most famous one. It provides the exact day (2 July 1505) when Luther, while travelling through a terrifying thunderstorm, vowed to commit his life to God. This is also true of another famous church leader, John Wesley, who became the founder of Methodism. On 21 May 1738 Wesley 'turned around' when he opened his Bible and read a message that spoke to him in a way God's Word had never spoken to him before. There are also people in our day and age who know exactly when their conversion took place. Some time ago I read the conversion story of Alvin Plantinga (born 1932), a Christian philosopher I referred to earlier in this book. One gloomy January evening Plantinga walked across the campus of Harvard University, where he was studying, and all of a sudden the doubts which had plagued him for a very long time were dissolved.

'It was dark, windy, raining, nasty. But suddenly it was as if the heavens opened; I heard, so it seemed, music of overwhelming power and grandeur and sweetness; there was light of unimaginable splendour and beauty; it seemed I could see into heaven itself; and I suddenly saw or perhaps felt with great clarity and persuasion and conviction that the Lord was really there and was all I had thought. The effects of this experience lingered for a long time: I was still caught up in arguments about the existence of God, but they often seemed to me merely academic, of little existential concern.'[206]

It must be admitted that this type of conversion story is not typical for most people of our postmodern generation who have 'turned around'. Their conversion typically is a process stretching over months or years, rather than the result of a sudden *aha-erlebnis*. The postmodern person may realize that her life is empty and unfulfilled. She may begin a search for meaning and may after much reading and thinking and talking with other genuine, authentic Christians, decide to take her leap of faith. Often she will begin to enjoy belonging to a community of faith even before she understands in any detail what that community believes.

A generation or so ago *believing* used to come before *belonging*. Today the order has been reversed: *belonging* usually precedes *believing*. This means that the conversion, or turning around, of postmodern people is generally the culmination of a long process, and often it is not easy to say when it started and when the turn around was complete. But at some point a clear decision must be made: Do I want to be a disciple of Jesus? Yes or No? Do I continue to see myself and my own concerns as the centre of my universe, or has Jesus Christ become the focal point of my existence?

Servants

Anyone who does any reading in the New Testament soon notices that Jesus carries a number of different titles. He is called our Saviour, but also the Messiah (a Hebrew word which is translated in Greek as 'Christos', 'the Christ', the Anointed One). Jesus is also referred to as our 'King' or as our 'High Priest', and as the 'Word'. Two additional very significant titles are 'Son of Man' and 'Son of God', which underline, respectively, Jesus' complete solidarity with the human race and his divine status. But there is one title which is in a class of its own – Jesus is also called the *Lord*. The title is extremely significant, for in the Graeco-Roman world this epithet was reserved for the Roman emperor, who not only claimed to be the absolute ruler in temporal affairs but also to posses divine status with all that implied. His subjects were required to worship him as their divine lord! The early Christians, however, were clear about their deepest allegiance, in spite of the immense dangers involved. They refused to worship the emperor as the ultimate source of authority. Not Caesar but Jesus Christ was their Lord.[207] Once we know this background, we are struck even more forcefully by the confession of Thomas. He was the last of the disciples to believe that Christ had indeed risen from the dead. But when he finally saw the light, all his doubt had dissipated, and he knew he stood face to face with his resurrected Master and exclaimed: 'My Lord and my God!'[208] He never again wavered from his service to his Lord.

It is important to introduce the terms 'serve' and 'servant' at this point. For, if Jesus Christ is our 'Lord', we are his 'servants'. This is, indeed, how the Bible repeatedly describes the followers of Jesus. Even the word 'slave' is used. Many Christians speak about 'serving' God without giving it a second thought. If you believe in God, you 'serve' him – it is as simple as that. The words, it seems, are almost fully interchangeable. And, in fact, in a sense they are. A genuine and profound belief in God will naturally translate itself into 'service'. But in reality this is not always what we see. Many people claim to believe in a higher being or power, or even the God of the Bible, but do not allow that belief to impact to any major degree on how they think and operate in their daily lives. There are plenty of examples of people whose beliefs – whether they are some vaguely held notions or ideas that have been shaped into a sophisticated theological system – do not lead to real service. That is, they do not in any significant manner change their deepest loyalties and commitments. The majority of the people around us may be religious but, unfortunately, their ultimate attachment is often to themselves rather than to Someone outside of themselves. They may even consider themselves as solid Christians, but if they were to engage in some honest introspection they would have to admit that material things, status or position, and relationships to people, are the driving forces in their lives. Many of those who claim to 'serve' God, in fact, primarily 'serve' themselves.

But, let's be honest: Who wants to be a servant? Whose ideal can it possibly be to serve someone else? Of course, we talk respectfully about various kinds of service. When enumerating the values we believe in, 'serving' our country is high on the list. We refer to our leaders in government as people who *serve* the nation. Pastors and other church leaders do not just work, they *serve*. In the area of economics we recognize that the *service*-industry is an ever-more important aspect of Western business life. And when retailers fail to provide good *service* to their customers their business will soon collapse.

To provide a service is something positive. But to *be* a servant? To constantly take orders from someone else, and have to do the bidding of a master, whose demands must be obeyed if disciplinary action is to be avoided – that is something else. Yes, we like to shop in places where we know we receive good, professional service. And we applaud people who show a high level of dedication to an ideal in their service to the nation, an organization, or the church. But we do not consider servility a positive attribute and a modern employer is not supposed to treat his employees as servants, whose opinions do not count and whose only role is blindly to do what is commanded.

In the late 1980s and early 1990s I lived in West Africa. One of the many things I had to get used to was having 'servants'. I must admit I adjusted to this new reality rather quickly. There is something to be said for having someone around – especially in a hot and humid climate – who cleans your car, looks after your garbage, and keeps your garden in good shape. And my wife was quite happy with the help she received in the home, in dealing with the laundry, the cooking and a host of other things which proved to be much more time-consuming in our new environment than they had been in our home country. I believe we treated the people who worked for us well. But deep down I always felt a sense of embarrassment. Why should other people serve us? What was so special about us that we should be in such a privileged position that we could hire the service of other human beings? And why would we be so lucky to enjoy the luxury of being exempt from so many menial duties? I must admit, nonetheless, that I was grateful that the roles were not reversed.

In the forty years of my church 'service', I have mostly been in positions where other people worked 'for' me. I have been in charge of church institutions or worked in church offices where a number of people had to work under my direction and responsibility. It is for others to say what kind of 'boss' I have been. Obviously, some relationships were better than others. I always tried very hard not to treat people with a sense of innate superiority, as if it was just natural that I would lead and they simply had to follow. But, at the same time, I must admit that I also appreciated the fact that I could delegate certain duties to others, and would not always gladly have exchanged roles with the members of my staff.

This chapter is about *service*, but it is about a special kind of service, quite different from what I just described. It is about the *kind of service we all owe to our Lord*. If our religion is to be genuine, and our allegiance is to be real, we must be servants. If we want to have a good understanding of what servanthood entails, we must first of all appreciate the enormous distance in status between the servant and the master. We must know our status before God. He is the majestic Creator of all that exists, while we are the creatures of his hands. He is eternal, without beginning and without ending, while the vast majority of us do not live beyond the age of 80 or 90. God is everywhere, while we are confined to one place at any given time. God knows everything, while the greatest scientist on earth knows only an infinitesimally small part of all there is to know. God is all-powerful, while we cannot even change the colour of our skin or fully ensure that we do not catch this year's variety of the flu.

God revealed himself in Jesus Christ as our *Lord* and Master, while calling us to be his *servants*. Some have tried to downplay the importance of this perspective. They maintain that people who have turned around and have truly focused their life on

God are no longer servants, but God's *friends*. God no longer sees us, they say, as his slaves, but as his friends or even as his children. On the surface there may be some biblical justification for this. After illustrating the closeness in his relationship with his followers through the image of the vine and the branches, Christ stated, 'I do no longer call you servants . . . instead, I have called you friends'.[209] But the biblical evidence as a whole suggests that we must not limit the definition of our relationship to God to one single term. This relationship is so wonderfully rich, and has such deep dimensions that we would get stuck in a caricature if we were to restrict it to just one image. When we focus here on the metaphor of *servanthood*, there is no explicit or implicit denial of the glorious fact that we are also God's friends or God's children. It is, rather, an emphatic insistence that our religion, our view of our relationship to God, is totally deficient if we forget or downsize this element of servanthood.

The Bible does not mince words, but calls a spade a spade. The most common word in the New Testament to refer to this servanthood is quite straightforward: we are God's *slaves*.[210] It almost seems politically incorrect to continue the use of this ugly word. Slavery is a crime against humanity. We can understand that the terrible past is still very much alive for the descendents of those who were sold like cattle to work on the white man's plantations. The blame for the institution of slavery, as it 'flourished' in the seventeenth, eighteenth and well into the nineteenth century, must be shared by Americans, Europeans and even some Africans. The former president of Senegal, Léopold Sédar Senghor (1906-2001), once remarked that he did not feel that any restitution ought to be paid to the descendants of African slaves, as many African chiefs were also quite eager to sell fellow-Africans to the colonial masters. As a Dutchman I realize with shame that my countrymen provided an important link in the slave-traffic between West Africa and the New World.

The essence of human slavery is that a person is treated as the property of someone else. The slave loses his autonomy, and becomes fully subject to the often capricious and cruel will of another person. No country today will officially acknowledge that slavery still exists within its borders. The tragic reality is that there are still places in the world where people are so dependent upon others, and so chained to an employer or a plot of land that they are slaves, if not in name then certainly in fact. Millions of people in developing countries, a large percentage of them under the age of 12, work in factories under conditions which are little better than slavery. A few years ago I visited a development project in a village in the Punjab province of Pakistan and was told that a family was so eager to have a latrine that in order to be able to pay their small contribution they were willing to sell their child for about 25 dollars!

So, against that backdrop, it stands to reason that we have a loathing for the word 'slave', and would hardly appreciate that label. To be called a 'slave!' There must be a less objectionable term. Well, yes, there is. We could use the word 'servant'. But that term does not sit well with us either. It is a word of the past. Take a look at the classified adds in the newspaper. Today, employers are not looking for servants, but for managerial assistants!

The entire idea of being a slave or a servant is contrary to our contemporary Western ethos. We do not instill in our children any aspirations to become someone's servant. We encourage them to do well in school, and get a degree, so that they can become leaders rather than servants. We want them to be successful, to climb the ladder of achievement, to make their mark and be masters of their own destiny. The idea of servanthood does not fit in this train of thought. But if we tie the biblical concept of servanthood too closely to our view of slavery as utter misery and degradation, we miss the mark. First of all, we would do well to study the institution of slavery as it existed in Bible times. We find that in the Old Testament era a slave could at times rise to a rather privileged status in a household and could be entrusted with considerable responsibilities. The example of Elimelech immediately springs to mind. Abraham trusted him to the extent that he sent him on a search for a suitable wife for his son.[211] And we immediately also think of Joseph, who became the manager of all Potiphar's affairs.[212]

Similarly, in New Testament times not all slaves would be treated badly. In fact, many slaves, when given the choice, opted to stay with their master rather than to be freed. So the very mention of words like slavery and servanthood may not have evoked as much negative feeling then as they do today. Anyway, the Bible uses the terminology of servanthood, when referring to our relationship to God, in rather a specific way. It does not for a moment suggest that to be a slave in God's service implies a loss of our individual freedom and personhood. It refers rather to a fundamental attitude. It points to what we consider as our highest goals, and to what we uphold as our highest values. It indicates where we have our deepest commitments.

Slavery or freedom?

The apostle Paul insisted that the church members ought to see him and his colleagues as servants of Christ.[213] Interestingly enough, he does not immediately define this servanthood only in terms of obedience, but rather in terms of having been entrusted with a sacred task. Too often many are inclined to think that being a slave or servant of Christ is first of all something negative – one must give up a myriad things; one must deny oneself all those elements of life that give joy and are of interest, and one must turn one's back on the challenges of this world. Following Christ, it is often thought, is giving up on friends, even relatives, and certainly on material things.[214] And if we get anything in exchange, it is the burden of a cross and a life of discomfort. [215] People point us to the statement in which Jesus warned his followers: 'Foxes have holes and birds of the air have nests, but the Son of man has no place to lay his head.'[216]

Sure enough, these and similar Bible texts do give food for thought and can only be ignored at our own spiritual peril. But the picture must be balanced by the glorious realization that it proves a tremendous blessing, both with regard to this life and to the life beyond this present world, if we are able to let go of things which may only give temporary pleasure but do not provide lasting satisfaction. The strange and paradoxical truth is that being a slave of Christ translates into a life of wonderful freedom, whereas many who claim to be totally free in the way they live and love, are in actual fact enslaved to habits, objects and attitudes with bonds that they are unable to break. Paul puts it like this: 'Thanks be to God that, though you used to be slaves to sin, you wholeheartedly obeyed the form of teaching to which you were entrusted. You have been set free from sin and have become slaves to righteousness.' [217] [Being set free to become slaves – this must be interesting news to postmodern people who thrive on paradoxes!]

It is not difficult to see the truth of what Paul is saying in the behaviour of many people around us. People can claim that they are free; that they can do whatever they want, while in reality they are unable to control their impulses and actions. Millions of people are addicted to alcohol or other drugs, and are unable to break away from their self-destructive habits. Many people are miserably enslaved to sex in all its lurid forms. They claim to enjoy their sexual freedom, but deep down they know their pleasures fail to fill the immense void within them, and they realize that they are being pulled ever deeper into empty and debasing experiments without the inner strength to turn away from their pitiful lifestyle. Modern slavery also comes in many other forms: television, computer games, lottery, sport, and, yes, work. This is the terrible plight of so many: They know what they should do and what they should no longer do. But they do not have the courage, the persistence or the moral strength, to make radical changes in their lives and to free themselves from the chains that keep them enslaved. Paul writes to the Roman believers about this ongoing tragedy: So often we know what to do, but do not have the stamina to follow the dictates of our conscience. Instead, we continue to do the things that we know we should not be engaged in. No human power is equal to that predicament. The apostle cries out: 'Who will deliver me from this awful situation?'[218] He knows that the solution must come from beyond ourselves. It is only through help from the Outside that we can exchange the 'slavery to sin' for 'slavery to righteousness'.[219]

It is not until we change our deepest loyalties and become servants of Christ that we find our true selves and discover our ultimate identity as creatures of the God of the universe. This wonderful kind of 'slavery', this voluntary service to God, is a holistic service that involves our entire being. This was already reflected in the Old Testament and reiterated in the New Testament by Jesus:

'Love the Lord your God *with all your heart and with all your soul and with all your strength*'. [220]

'Love the Lord your God *with all your heart and with all your soul and with all your mind*'.[221]

Making the most of our gifts

When we use the term 'pilgrimage' to describe our journey of faith discovery and to talk about the step-by-step-process we have followed, we imply that things take time. Turning around is a matter of deciding on our direction and orientation, but reaching the ultimate goal is a different matter. It will take time, and perseverance. It requires a constant vision and a careful following of the divinely provided roadmap. The image of the 'new birth' teaches us the same basic truth. A baby must grow up and mature. It will need the right kind of food for the various stages of its growth.[222] We must 'grow in the faith and knowledge of our Lord and Saviour Jesus Christ.'[223] There will be moments of doubt and anxiety. But by not giving up and keeping our eyes fixed on our Master, we can overcome any such hurdles. At times our journey of faith will resemble a battle. We are admonished to 'fight the good fight' with all the spiritual weapons we have at our disposal.[224] Reading the Bible and meditating upon the Word of God, in addition to a disciplined prayer life, are essential elements in the lives of those who have committed themselves to serving God.

As we travel our spiritual journey, and fight the good fight, and as our faith matures, we are not left to our own devising. We are being provided with an array of gifts and capabilities.[225] Admittedly, we are gifted in various ways. But all of us have at least some gifts and abilities and are to use them to our full potential. Regrettably, many people have wasted much of their lives and never did what they could have done if only their abilities had been recognized, by themselves and by others! However, there are also many who did clearly recognize their giftedness in a number of areas, but failed to develop it. There are but few natural talents which are so distinct that they do not need nurture or development. Most of us progress by using and perfecting our skills, and must sharpen our gifts through a long process of learning by trial and error and constant practice. This requires discipline – and in particular self-discipline.

Discipline

People who achieve great things are usually disciplined people. President Roosevelt once remarked that one of the things which destroys life is soft living without any discipline. Lenin, the architect of the Russian Revolution of 1918, may have overstated his case, but his point was well taken when he said: 'Give me a handful of disciplined people who dedicate their lives to me and I will control the world'.[226] We see the sportsmen and sportswomen in their brief moment of glory on the Olympic podium when they receive their gold medal, but, when asked, most will tell you that their achievement is the result of long years of relentless training. We enjoy a symphony in a large concert hall, but while we applaud the musicians and the conductor we realize in the back of our minds that the performance was not the result of a chance encounter of a hundred or so naturally talented musicians. Every one of them has spent years in learning how to play the violin, the oboe, or the clarinet, and the orchestra as a whole spends far more time practising than performing. An author may be blessed with an unusual linguistic and stylistic ability, but his first book is not usually his best book: as he wrestles with plots and words he grows in his craft. Even a popular preacher who has the gift of communicating with his audience will need to spend long hours reading, thinking and writing before he can deliver his message, and will further improve his skills as he continues to put a lot of time into his preparations. And we all know that most of us must spend considerable time at our keyboards before the computer does what we intend it to do.

To be disciplined does not mean to become like a robot. Learning and perfecting a skill demands focus, but should never become an obsession. It demands time, but it would be wrong to let it absorb all our free moments, so that there is no longer any space in our schedule for pleasure and adventure, and for the unexpected. Discipline is first of all a matter of establishing priorities. What do we consider as really important? How can we subordinate the lesser to the greater? Discipline has everything to do with choice. You may be a person with a natural curiosity who wants to know what is going on, but you cannot hope to see everything there is to see. You may be a voracious reader who wants to keep up with modern literature or with the publications in your field of specialty. But you cannot possibly read everything the publishers put out. You may enjoy travelling, but most likely you will never have enough time and money to see all the places in this world that tickle your imagination. We are all limited in the amount of time we have, the amount of energy we possess, and in numerous other aspects.

This is not as tragic as it may seem. Not every experience adds to our happiness and maturity. There are many things in our sinful world which are not worth experiencing. As we already noted in the previous chapter, many things have a minus sign attached to them instead of a plus sign, and only detract from our personal fulfilment and enjoyment of life rather than adding to these. Not everything there is to see is worth seeing, and not everything there is to hear or read is worth hearing or reading. Not every place is worth visiting. Besides, we do well to consider quality before quantity. We must learn to enjoy thoroughly the few things we carefully select to see, hear, read, visit, etc. If we succeed along this path, we will have the time and energy to develop our gifts and talents as we should.

Discipline involves a number of principles. Firstly, it is only as we are able to discipline ourselves in the smaller things of life that we can tackle more formidable challenges. If I do not succeed in establishing a degree of order in my daily schedule, and in the environment in which I work and live, how can I expect to write a dissertation or manage a substantial project successfully, lead a group of other people, or become skilled at the saxophone? This is not just common sense, but also happens to be a sound biblical principle: 'Whoever can be trusted with very little can also be trusted with much!'[227]

Secondly, we must resist the temptation always to go for the easiest solutions to the issues and assignments we are facing. Of course, there are times when an easy solution to a problem that has been looming large in our minds stares us in the face. Sheer unbelief that things, for a change, could be easy, may lead us to ignore the quick solution and search unnecessarily for a more complicated route. But, generally speaking, when we are looking for shortcuts and easy answers, we tend to ignore vital aspects and will have to be content with only partial solutions. If we are faced with a complex problem or a significant challenge, we must have the discipline to analyse what we have in front of us and to develop a strategy for dealing with the issue. We will determine whether we have what it takes, whether we need to acquire or perfect certain extra skills, and to what extent we will have to rely on the expertise of others.

Thirdly – and this is closely linked to what we just discussed – we need to have ideals, goals, and objectives. And we must have some sort of programme or strategy to achieve those goals and ideals. That is true of any aspect of life: for our work, our studies, our hobbies, our home and our garden. But it equally applies to our family life and our wider social relationships, to our church involvement and our spiritual well-being and growth. It applies, for example, also to our prayer life and Bible reading. Making plans and listing goals is, however, one thing; to follow through on our plans and actually achieve what we set out to do is something else. It demands that we make a conscious use of the special gifts we have, but also that we discipline ourselves to keep those plans and goals in focus and work towards a gradual realisation.

Fourthly, we must ever remember that if something is worth doing, it is worth doing it well. It always mystifies me how people can be content with mediocre work and can live with a multitude of unfinished projects and be satisfied with a level of performance they know is far below their ability. Yes, it takes discipline, but it creates deep and lasting satisfaction if you deliver a product to the highest possible perfection. When we see a work by Rembrandt or Michelangelo, we admire the superb skills of these great master painters. But modern technology enables the specialist to discover some of the details of the genesis of these monuments of art. Often large sections of the canvas were repainted more than once or twice, figures were removed or added, facial expressions or body postures were radically changed, before the artist was satisfied with his work. It is reported that Ernest Hemingway rewrote the last chapter of his famous novel *Farewell to Arms* well over twenty times before he felt he had properly finished the book. Of course, there comes the time when we must move on to the next project, and we may occasionally have to be content with a standard that is less than perfect. But it remains true that that if something is worth doing, it is worth doing it to the very best of our ability.

Finally, discipline presupposes a willingness to sacrifice. If you want to be good at something, you may have to forego other things. To reach peak sporting condition will demand strenuous exercise and saying a conscious 'no' to those things which are a threat to physical fitness. Developing a musical talent will demand discipline and perseverance, and may often force us to let go of other favourite activities. If we want to excel, there is usually a price to pay. And that applies in a very special way also to our life of faith and service.

Fully Committed

Becoming and being a Christian is the easiest thing in the world. God provides everything for us. He created us with the innate ability to search and find him. He revealed himself to us through the Bible and, even more miraculously, in Jesus Christ. He dealt with our sin problem, established a community where we can be together with fellow believers and has equipped us to live the life of faith. The Christian fully depends on divine grace. 'For it is by grace that you have been saved, through faith – and this not from yourself, it is the gift of God.'[228]

But the German theologian Dietrich Bonhoeffer, who was killed by the Nazis just months before World War II ended, warned that this wonderful grace, although it is totally *free*, is not *cheap*. 'For God so loved the world' that he gave what was dearest to him: Jesus Christ.[229] And although, on the one hand, becoming a Christian is the easiest thing in the world, it is, at the same time, also a momentous challenge. Bonhoeffer wrote in his book *The Cost of Discipleship*, about this contradictory challenge the followers of Christ face:

'The disciple is dragged out of his relative security into a life of absolute insecurity (that is, in truth, into the absolute security and safety of the fellowship of Jesus), from a life which is observable and calculable (it is, in fact, incalculable) into a life where everything is unobservable and fortuitous (that is, into one that is necessary and calculable), out of the realm of the finite (which is, in truth, the infinite) into the real of the infinite possibilities (which is the one liberating reality).'[230]

You may have to read these words a few times before their significance sinks in. When I think about these words I feel like the disciples who wondered whether they would ever make it. After Christ had challenged a rich man to change his lifestyle radically, the disciples asked their Master in dismay: But if you require that kind of drastic turn around, 'who can then be saved?' The answer was as encouraging then, as it is for us today: 'With man this is impossible, but with God all things are possible.'[231] J. Heinrich Arnold's comment brings it home to us:

'A promise made to God cannot be made on the strength of human faithfulness. We must depend on God's faithfulness. No one is strong enough in his own strength to endure, for instance, what early Christian martyrs and others throughout history endured; but God is faithful. If we give ourselves to him, his angels will fight for us.'[232]

So, in a way, it's easy to start and to continue the pilgrimage of faith. *It is free, but at the same time it takes all we have and are.* It requires full and enduring commitment. I cannot find any better words than these which I recently came across:

'I've got news for you. True Christianity, courageous Christianity – the kind the apostles Paul and Peter and thousands of other early Christians preached – isn't for wimps. It's not for the faint-hearted, the lukewarm, the moderately committed, or the occasional churchgoer. It's for the passionate, the ones with the courage to say, 'I believe God, and I will dedicate my every waking hour to his purpose, no matter what it costs.'[233]

Chapter ten

Mission

Most companies and organizations have developed mission statements to summarize in just a few words what they want to achieve and how they intend to achieve it. The worldwide Coca Cola imperium describes its mission as ensuring that its product will be within the reach of every person on planet earth.[234] Anyone who has done any serious travelling will admit that the Coca Cola people have done extremely well. Even in distant, virtually inaccessible places in developing countries, where the mail service does not reach and the most basic elements of health care are unknown, Coca Cola has somehow penetrated.

Mission statements are important. The drafting process helps people to determine what their ultimate goal is, and seeing it daily in front of them helps them to remain focused on their task. Most church organizations nowadays also have mission statements, the denomination to which I belong (the Seventh-day Adventist Church) not excluded. But, important though that may be to me and all who belong to this fast growing movement, it is merely a contemporary rewording of the first mission statement, which was issued almost two thousand years ago. This original mission statement is often referred to as the *Great Gospel Commission* and is found in its fullest version in the final verses of the gospel of Matthew:

'Therefore go and make disciples of all nations, baptizing them in the name of the Father and of the Son and of the Holy Spirit, and teaching them to obey everything I have commanded you. And surely I am with you always, to the very end of the age.'[235]

Go, make disciples, baptize, teach. That is the assignment. What is the target group? It is as inclusive as that of the Coca Cola company: all nations (literally: all ethnic groups). And what is the duration of the campaign? From around the year 31AD to the very end of history.

The immediate audience of the original mission statement of the Jesus movement was a group of eleven men (the twelve disciples, minus Judas who committed suicide after his betrayal of Christ). In terms of human resources the mission seemed doomed. But, miraculously, it was a tremendous success from the very beginning. This was not due to the exceptional creativity, the immensity of material resources and the national and international network those eleven men brought to the job. They were mostly simple, uneducated men, mostly fishermen by trade. But they had received the most exclusive private tutoring that has ever been available. They had been with the Lord of the universe for over three years. Even that was not enough, however. They were to wait in Jerusalem until they would be further, supernaturally, equipped for their task. Ten days after the resurrected Christ had left this earth, the tiny workforce was touched by divine power in a manner that all who were present in Jerusalem could see and hear. As a result their first public campaign resulted in thousands of accessions to the newly established Christian church.[236]

From that moment onwards the growth of the Christian church was unstoppable. Have a look at a biblical atlas (your Bible may have some charts in the back) and you will be amazed about the extensive travelling of the disciples – who were called *apostles*, that is: 'those who are sent'. Paul, who soon joined the apostles, founded churches all over the Mediterranean world within about thirty years. Before the end of the first century the message of Jesus Christ had spread over the entire ancient world. And the church kept growing. We have documented evidence of a Christian presence in France from the second century onwards, as well as in England from the early third century. We know that Christianity soon spread along the North African coast and to the East, at least as far away as India.

This is not a book about church history. If you want to know more about the history of Christian missions, go to your library which will have several good books on the topic. It is fascinating to read about the missionaries who came from Ireland and Scotland and travelled to many areas of Europe. And about the vast numbers of missionaries who, in later times, left for South- and Inter-America, and to China and other places in Asia. In all honesty we must admit that some of their missionary methods left, at times, much to be desired, but at the same time we cannot fail to notice the enormous and sustained outburst of faith, heroism and dedication. When Protestantism came on the scene, it took the new movement a while before it embarked on a worldwide effort to spread the good news. The nineteenth century saw the beginning of the era of modern missions, with a particular focus on Africa. This was also the time when the Bible societies, as we now know them, were organized, and the challenge of translating the Bible into thousands of languages and dialects was seriously undertaken.

The increase in the absolute number of Christians is very encouraging – from roughly half a billion in 1900 to just over 2 billion in 2004. The increase in the number of Bible translations is also a matter of great satisfaction. The Bible is easily the most translated book in the world. It is found it its entirety or in part in 2,355 of the approximately 6,500 languages that exist and some additional 600 translation projects are under way.

The Bible is, in theory, available in whole or in part to roughly 98 per cent of the world's population. That does not mean, however, that almost all people in the world (if they are literate) do actually read the Bible. And the mission of communicating the Christian gospel is far from completed. In fact, statistics tell us that the percentage of Christians in the world has remained rather static for quite some time, at a little more than 30 per cent.

The world's population has grown dramatically, but the ratio of Christians to the world's population has remained about the same for over a century. In spite of all the resources Christians collectively have (their accumulated income has been estimated at over 16 trillion dollars); in spite of a total of 3.6 million Christian congregations worldwide; in spite of hundreds of missionary organizations which employ over 300,000 missionaries, and in spite of the advanced print and audiovisual media that are now available, the Christian message is still not heard in hundreds of millions of homes around the globe.[237] We also need to note that the centre of Christianity is slowly shifting from the North to the South. Africa and the Americas are slowly becoming the main centres of the Christian world, with large concentrations of Christians also in parts of Asia, while Christianity in the traditionally Christian West is slowly being eroded by secularism and non-Christian influences.[238]

Many of the over two billion non-Christians in the world are so by choice, and that choice must, of course, be respected. Many may, however, never have had the chance to evaluate their beliefs seriously, and might well become Christians once they really understand the uniqueness of the Christian message. They need to hear what Christianity has to offer. Of course, they must not be pushed and manipulated, and must at all times remain free to make their own religious choice and, then, to follow the dictates of their own conscience. But roughly one in every four people on this planet, it is estimated, has never heard of the Christian God and is totally unaware of who and what Jesus Christ is. About two billion people alive today have not yet had the opportunity to choose for or against the Christian God. How can that be? If Coca Cola can acquaint virtually all people around the world with their product, what's wrong with the 3.6 million Christian congregations and their two billion members? Why haven't they yet reached every city, town and village in the world?

Apparently, much of Christianity is not what it should be. A large percentage of it is without real zeal and power. Much of it is tradition and culture. It is hard to tell how many of those two billion people who say they are Christians only see the inside of a church at Christmas time or when invited to a wedding or a funeral. Some hardly support the mission of the church, if they do so at all. Hundreds of millions of Christians spend more of their money on chewing gum than they contribute to the mission of their church. However, I know I must be careful in making sweeping judgements, for there are also hundreds of millions of Christians around the world who serve their Lord with total dedication, and are more than generous in their support for the work of the church at home and abroad. Yet, it must be underlined: Mission is a vital concept. When a church organization loses its missionary zeal it has lost the reason for its existence and will soon lose its very life.

This is one of the reasons why I have chosen to belong to a church that is keenly mission-driven. Because it is focused on mission, it is a vibrant and growing church. I have been a member since my youth and I have stayed with my church. I remember the announcement that my church had reached the one million member mark. As I write, the Seventh-day Adventist church has over 14 million baptized members and there are possibly about twice as many who worship in Adventist churches and see themselves as part of the Adventist family. Together the members of my church donate annually a few billion dollars to the mission of their church. And this emphasis on mission makes a difference. While the ratio of Christians to the world's population has remained static, there is now one Adventist to every 468 people in the world, while only 50 years ago the ratio was one to over 3,000!

All of us individually can make a difference to the mission of the church. Some us can go to other parts of the world and participate in the actual preaching of the gospel or take part in other types of mission projects. Many more of us can give generously (bring a real 'sacrifice' in monetary terms), and all of us can pray for the various aspects of the preaching of the message of forgiveness and abundant life in Christ.

But it is especially close to home where we really need to make a difference. Like the apostles in the story of the Book of Acts, we are called to be 'witnesses' of what God has done for us in Jesus Christ.[239] Often we will have to be content with being silent witnesses. That is not so bad, for deeds often speak louder than words, anyway. But when the opportunity arises, we must be outspoken and tell people with conviction, and unashamedly, of the hope that is in us. This may not always be easy and may take its toll. It is not without deep significance that the original word in the New Testament that is usually translated as 'witness', also has the meaning of 'martyr'!

If you have come this far, and taken the consecutive steps of this journey of discovery, you must not stop here. Your commitment to the faith you have found must find expression in personal involvement in the mission that God has entrusted to all believers. If you have heard the good news for yourself and have taken the leap of faith, you will be eager to talk with others about it. This used to be quite difficult. The Western world, in particular Western Europe, went through a period in which talking about your religion was a greater taboo than talking about your sex life. It was simply not done. Religion was private. This is rapidly changing. It is OK again to talk about religion and people no longer look at you with pity when you say you believe in God. Spirituality is firmly back on the postmodern agenda. This, however, does not mean that it is easy to convince people of the 'truth' of the Christian message, as found in the Bible. The postmodern person picks and chooses what she will believe and does not easily accept that your 'truth' is better than her 'truth'. Yet, there are far more opportunities for Christian witness than just a decade or so ago. Postmodernism has changed the context in which we are called to witness.

If we are fully committed in our faith in God and have made the conscious decision to be a disciple and servant of the Lord, we cannot and will not dodge our mission. We will do all we can to point our partner, our children, our relatives, our friends and colleagues to the Source of meaning and inspiration we have found. We will do our utmost to lead them through the kind of process that I have outlined in this book. Be prepared: you may have to be patient. And make sure that you use language others can understand. It may take a long time before you see them make the decisive 'turn around' and before they are ready for the final commitment.

But remember two things. Firstly, postmodern people are

looking for more than carefully crafted arguments. They want to see more than well-oiled ecclesiastical machinery. They want to see real people who consistently live their faith. They will be impressed by authentic Christians who are in reality what they profess to be. If you want to share your faith, make sure that the people around you can see that your faith makes a difference in your life. Do not just talk about the full life that Christ offers, but model that abundant life in simplicity and with integrity. And secondly, try to bring people into a community of believers. It is essential that they *belong* as they begin to *believe*.

Remember, I warned you when you started this book, that this would not be a book you can read noncommittally and then just put on the shelf. It demands action. It leaves you with a tremendous challenge. Find the meaning for your life and take the leap of faith. In other words: *Find God and yourself*. Find hope and true rest. Be forgiven and learn how to forgive. Choose to be a disciple of Christ and a steward of what God has given you. Commit yourself completely to the Lord. And, then, start the cycle again. Look at the people around you. Many miss the sense of meaning that is now yours. They have not yet taken the leap of faith that landed you in a totally new world. They need to be started on that journey of discovery. Point them the way and stay close to them. Help others to find the Truth, while you yourself continue 'to grow in the faith and the knowledge of our Lord and Saviour Jesus Christ'.[240]

I have shared my faith with you who have read this book. I have chosen to *write* about my faith. I believe I am better at writing than at preaching. This is how I prefer to tell others about my faith. Because that's where, I think, I have some talent. I want to use it the best I can while I 'serve' my Lord. I challenge you to discover and use your gifts and witness to your faith as effectively as you can where you are. God is asking a lot. But somehow he has equipped all of us with what it takes to be a disciple, a servant, and a witness of our Lord!

References

1. In recent times Christians have intensely discussed whether God has any gender and whether 'he' should be regarded as 'male' or as 'female'. We shall return to that issue in the next chapter. In this book I shall use masculine language when referring to God, even though I realize this is inadequate.

2. A. Camus, The Myth of Sisyphus (London, UK: Penguin, 1955), p. 11.

3. The more 'advanced' reader who is interested in a thorough discussion of the two approaches outlined in this chapter will find this in Nancy Murphy, *Beyond Liberalism and Fundamentalism* (Harrisburg, PA: Trinity Press International, 1996). I am indebted to this author for the terminology of 'inside out' and 'outside in'.

4. See Thomas Kuhn, *The Structure of Scientific Revolutions*, 2nd ed. (Chicago: The University of Chicago Press, 1970). Kuhn introduces the concept of *paradigm shifts* as he explains the appearance of these new scientific umbrellas.

5. For a short survey of relevant issues by an Adventist author, see Norman R. Gulley, 'Evolution: A Theory in Crisis', in John T. Baldwin, ed., *Creation: Catastrophe & Calvary* (Hagerstown, MD: Review and Herald Publishing Association, 2000), pp. 124-158. For a fuller treatment, see e.g. Colin Mitchell, *Creationism Revisited* (Grantham, UK: Stanborough Press, 1999); Michael Denton, *Evolution: A Theory in Crisis* (Chevy Chase, MD: Adler & Adler, 1996 ed.; and Ariel Roth, *Origins: Linking Science and Scripture* (Hagerstown, MD: Review and Herald Publishing Association, 1998).

6. Kurt O. Wise, 'The Origin of Life's Major Groups', in J.P. Moreland, ed., *The Creation Hypothesis* (Downers Grove, Il: InterVarsity Press, 1994), p. 231.

7. Published: New York: Simon and Schuster, 1988, p. 203.

8. Stephen C. Meijer, 'Evidence for Design in Physics and Biology', pp. 53-111, in: Michael J. Behe, et. al., eds. *Science and Evidence for Design in the Universe* (San Francisco, CA: Ignatius Press, 2000), p. 61.

9. Gulley, *op. cit.*, 142.

10. Mooreland, *op. cit.*, 228-231.

11. Michael J. Behe, 'Design at the Foundation of Life', pp. 113-129 in Michael J. Behe, *op. cit.*, pp. 117f.

12. Ariel A. Roth, *Origins – Linking Science and Scripture*. (Hagerstown, MD; Review and Herald Publishing Association, 1998), p. 77.

13. Alan Bloom, *The Closing of the American Mind* (New York, NY: Simon & Schuster, Inc., 1987), 25.

14. Robert C. Greer, *Mapping Postmodernism: A Survey of Christian Options* (Downers Grove, IL: InterVarsity Press, 2003), p. 228.

15. Cf. the title of his book: Douglas Groothuis: *Truth Decay: Defending Christianity against the Challenges of Postmodernism* (Downers Grove, IL: InterVarsity Press, 2000).

16. Groothuis, *op. cit*, p. 175ff.

17. For an enlightening discussion, see Nancy Murphy, *Beyond Liberalism and Fundamentalism. How Modern and Postmodern Philosophy Set the Theological Agenda* (Harrisburg, PA: Trinity Press International, 1996), pp. 85-109.

18. Greer, *op. cit.*, p. 41.

19 Groothuis, *op. cit.*, p. 166.
20 The sections are named after their authors, Matthew, Mark, Luke and John. I suggest that a novice in Bible reading starts with the Gospel of Mark.
21 Groothuis, *op. cit.*, 179ff
22 Alvin Plantinga, *Warranted Christian Belief* (New York, Oxford: Oxford University Press, 2000), pp. 192-198.
23 Hans Küng, *Credo* (London: SMC Press, 1993 ed.), p. 14.
24 Anny Matti, *Moeite met God* (Kampen, the Netherlands: J. H. Kok Uitgeversmaatschappij, 1991), p. 48.
25 J. P. Tillich, *Dynamics of Faith*, (New York 1957), p. 1.
26 Hebrews 11:1.
27 Plantinga, *op. cit.*, 217-222.
28 Kung, *op. cit.*, pp. 7-11
29 *Ibid.*, p. 11.
30 John Calvin, one of the key leaders of 16th century Protestantism, used the term *sensus divinatis*, i.e. an inner awareness of the divine presence.
31 Romans 7:15.
32 Plantinga, *op. cit.* 207.
33 *Ibid.*, p. 184f.
34 H. C. Rümke, *Karakter en Aanleg in Verband met het Ongeloof* (Kampen: Kok Agora, 2003 ed.).
35 *Ibid.*, pp. 29-34.
36 Romans 1:20.
37 Ephesians 2:8.
38 Fritz Guy, *Thinking Theologically* (Berrien Springs, MI: Andrews University Press, 1999). p. 5.
39 Rümke, *op. cit.*, pp. 37f.
40 Robert C. Greer, *Mapping Postmodernism: A Survey of Christian Options* (Downers Grove, IL: InterVarsity Press, 2003), pp. 172ff.
41 Plantinga, *op. cit.*, p. 200.
42 Mark 9:24.
43 1 Corinthians 13:13.
44 Luke 21:26.
45 1 Thessalonians 4:13.
46 Rudolph W. Giuliani (with Ken Kurson), *Leadership* (London: TimeWarner, 2002 ed.), pp. 155ff.
47 Romans 8:24.
48 Exodus 3:14.
49 1 John 4:18.

50 John 3:16.

51 See e.g. Revelation 12:7ff which speaks of a 'war in heaven' that preceded the tragedy on earth. Two other highly symbolic passages also indicate that more was involved than just a human dimension: Isaiah 14:12-15; Ezekiel 28:11-19.

52 John 4:24.

53 Hebrews 2:7.

54 Genesis 1:27.

55 Matthew 25:14-30; Luke 19:12-27.

56 1 Corinthians 15:12-19.

57 Deuteronomy 31:16; 1 Kings 2:10; Job 14:12: Daniel 12:2; Matthew 9:24; 27:51, 52; John 11:11; Acts 7:60; 1 Corinthians 15: 18, 51; 1 Thessalonians 4:13.

58 1 Thessalonians 4:13.

59 Jack Provonsha, *Dood: zijn of niet-zijn* (Uitgeverij Veritas: Alphen aan den Rijn, 1983), p.70.

60 Quoted by Hans Küng, *Eeuwig Leven* (Hilversum: Gooi en Sticht, 1983), p. 128.

61 1 Corinthians 6:14.

62 1 John 3:2.

63 Philippians 2:7.

64 Interview in *Time*, 24 november 1967.

65 Quoted in Os Guinness, *The Dust of Death* (Leicester: InterVarsity Press, 1973), p. 13.

66 1 Corinthians 15:19.

67 John 14:3.

68 Revelation 22:20.

69 Titus 2:13.

70 Revelation 21:1.

71 1 John 3:2.

72 Revelation 21:4.

73 Revelation 21:8.

74 The Bible uses, in fact, this very term in connection of evil, and refers to the 'mystery of iniquity'. See 2 Thessalonians 2:7.

75 Romans 3:10; Psalm 14:3.

76 Romans 3:23.

77 See e.g. John 12:31; 1 John 5:19; 1 John 3:8; Job 1:6; Colossians 2:15.

78 1 Timothy 3:16.

79 Charles Scriven, *The Demons Have Had It: A Theological ABC* (Nashville, TN: Southern Publishing Association, 1976), pp. 62-63.

80 *Ibid.*, p. 62.

81 Isaiah 59:2.

82 Romans 14:23.

83 1 Kings 8:39.
84 See Exodus 20:1-17 for the best known version; for a slightly different version, which, however, enshrines the same ten basic principles, see Deuteronomy 5:6-21.
85 1 John 3:4.
86 Revelation 20:6.
87 John 3:16.
88 1 John 4:10.
89 I suggest you start with Mark 14:1 and continue until the end of the book of Mark.
90 Richard Rice, *The Reign of God* (Berrien Springs, MI: Andrews University Press, 1997 ed), p. 191.
91 John 1:29.
92 1 John 2:2.
93 1 Peter 1:18, 19.
94 Ephesians 1:7.
95 1 Corinthians 6:20.
96 Mark 10:45.
97 See Romans chapters 2-6.
98 See Isaiah 53:2-12.
99 Rice, *op. cit.*, p. 198.
100 Scriven, *op. cit.*, p. 59.
101 Micah 7:18.
102 Jeremiah 31:34.
103 Matthew 6:12.
104 Matthew 18:21.
105 Philip Yancey, *What's So Amazing Grace About Grace?* (Grand Rapids, MI: Zondervan Publishing House, 1997), pp. 37-38.
106 Nan Chase, 'Ancient Wisdom' in *Hemispheres* (in-flight magazine of United Airlines), July 1997.
107 Adrian Verbree, *Eclipse – Verslag van een Burn-out* (Barneveld, the Netherlands: Plateau, 2003).
108 Matthew 11:28.
109 Hebrews 4:9.
110 See J.H. Meesters, *Op Zoek naar de Oorsprong van de Sabbat* (Assen: van Gorcum, 1966), passim.
111 Genesis 2:1-3.
112 Marva J. Dawn, *Keeping the Sabbath Wholly.* (Grand Rapids, William B. Eerdmans Publishing Company, 1996 ed.), p. 19.
113 Jon Dybdahl, *Exodus – The Abundant Life Bible Amplifier* (Boise ID: Pacific Press Publishing Association, 1994), p. 186

[114] Wayne Muller, *Sabbath: Finding Rest, Renewal and Delight in our Busy Lives* (New York: Bantam Books, 2000 ed.), pp. 31, 32.

[115] Mark 2:27.

[116] Luke 4:16.

[117] Matthew 9:14-17; Mark 2:18-3:6; 3:1-4; 7:1-7; 15:2; Luke 5:33-39; 6:1-11; 14:1-6; 23:54-24:1. John 5:6-8. See also Matthew 19:16, 17.

[118] Marva J. Dawn, *op. cit.*, pp. 138-139, 203.

[119] Richard Rice, *The Reign of God* (Berrien Springs, MI: Andrews University Press, 1997 ed., p. 403.

[120] They form, however, a sizable and growing community. Some 20-25 million people in the world now refer to themselves as Seventh-day Adventists and that number is rapidly growing.

[121] For information about the historical process of the change from Sabbath to Sunday, see e.g. K. A. Strand, ed., *The Sabbath in Scripture and History* (Washington, DC: Review and Herald Publishing House, 1982); R. Bruinsma, *The Day God Created* (Grantham, UK: Stanborough Press, Ltd, 1992).

[122] James 2:10

[123] Exodus 16:4.

[124] Ezekiel 20:12, 20.

[125] Revelation 12:17.

[126] Jon Paulien, *What the Bible Says about the End-time* (Hagerstown, MD: Review and Herald Publishing Association, 1994), p. 127.

[127] Robert Banks, *Redeeming the Routines: Bringing Theology to Life* (Grand Rapids, MI: Baker Academic, 1993), p. 73.

[128] Mike Regele and Mark Schulz, *Death of the Church* (Grand Rapids, MI: Zondervan Publishing House, 1995), p. 51

[129] Matthew 4:1-11; Mark 1:35.

[130] Genesis 2:18.

[131] See Romans 10, 11.

[132] Luke 22:20.

[133] Matthew 28:16-20; Acts 1:8.

[134] Acts 11:26.

[135] Richard Rice, *The Reign of God* (Berrien Springs, MI: Andrews University Press, 1997 ed.), p. 209.

[136] 1 Corinthians 1:1-3; 3; 6.

[137] Matthew 16:16-20.

[138] The question as to whether, or to what extent, the earliest Christian communities had female leadership remains a debated issue. See Robert M. Johnston, 'Ministry in the New Testament and in the Early Church', in: Nancy Vyhmeister, ed., *Women in Ministry –Biblical and Historical Perspectives* (Berrien Springs, MI: Andrews University Press, 1998), p. 51f .

[139] Matthew 25: 1-13; Revelation 21:2.

[140] See Revelation 12.

[141] Revelation 17.

[142] 1 Corinthians 12:12-31.

[143] 1 Corinthians 12:1-11.

[144] Ephesians 4:11-13.

[145] See Romans 6:1-10.

[146] Mark 1:9-11.

[147] Matthew 28:19,20.

[148] John 3:23.

[149] 1 Corinthians 11:23-26.

[150] John 13: 1-17.

[151] E.G. White, *Testimonies to Ministers* (Mountain View, CA: Pacific Press Publishing Association, 1923,), p. 15.

[152] Richard Rice, *op. cit.*, 205.

[153] Hebrews 10:25.

[154] Romans 8:29.

[155] Brian D. McLaren, *A New Kind of Christian: A Tale of Two Friends on a Spiritual Journey*. San Francisco, CA: Jossey Bass, 2001, p. 155.

[156] Michael Riddell, *Threshold of the Future: Reforming the Church in the Post-Christian West* (London, SPCK, 1998), p. 62.

[157] John Drane, *Faith in a Changing Culture: Creating Churches for the Next Century* (London: Marshall Pickering, 1997 ed.) p. 201.

[158] Lee Strobel, *Inside the Mind of Unchurched Harry & Mary* (Grand Rapids, MI: Zondervan Publishing House, 1993), p. 120.

[159] See Jeremy Langford, *God Moments – Why Faith Really Matters to a New Generation* (Maryknoll, NY: Orbis Books, 2001), pp. 67-72.

[160] C.S. Lewis, *Mere Christianity* (New York, MacMillan, Collier Books, 1943), 75.

[161] John 8:32.

[162] John 10:10.

[163] See the section in Luke 14 which deals with the costs of being a disciple (vs. 25-35).

[164] John 8:31.

[165] 19:11-27.

[166] See the *New Living Translation*.

[167] Genesis 1:28.

[168] Genesis 2:19.

[169] Genesis 2:15.

[170] R. Scott Rodin, *Stewards of the Kingdom – A Theology of Life in All Its Fullness* (Downers Grove, Il: InterVarsity Press, 2000), p. 144.

[171] For the definition of 'sin', see chapter 5.

[172] *Greening the Christian Millennium* (Dublin: Dominican Publications, 1999), p. 81.

[173] Robert Wuthnow, *God and Mammon in America* (New York: Free Press, 1994), p. 16.

[174] *Fifty Simple Things You Can Do to Save the World* (Berkeley, CA: The Earth Works Group, 1989), p. 20.

[175] Ellen G. White, *Testimonies to the Church*, vol. 2, p. 273.

[176] Leo R. van Dolson and J. Robert Spangler, *Healthy, Happy, Holy* (Washington, DC: Review and Herald Publishing Association, 1975), p. 44.

[177] 1 Corinthians 6:19.

[178] See Leviticus 11-16.

[179] Reinder Bruinsma, *Matters of Life and Death* (Boise, ID: Pacific Press Publishing Association, 2000), p. 132.

[180] Exodus 23:25, 26; Deuteronomy 5:33.

[181] Van Dolson and Spangler, *op. cit.*, p. 34.

[182] Kathleen H. Liwidjaja Kuntaraf, 'Healthy Choices and Living Options', in *Dialogue*, vol. 12, no. 1 (2000), p. 14.

[183] It should be noted that Latter-day Saints (Mormons) also live longer than the average population. They share a number of health principles with Seventh-day Adventists.

[184] Psalm 139:14.

[185] Luke 12:23.

[186] See e.g. John 2:1-11; Luke 5:29;

[187] The English title of the book is *The Protestant Work Ethic and the Spirit of Capitalism*. A current edition is published by Routledge (London, 2001).

[188] Ecclesiastes 3:1-8, 17.

[189] Matthew 22;37.

[190] Mike Nappa, *The Courage to Be a Christian* (West Monroe, Louisiana: 2001), pp. 161, 162.

[191] Acts 20:35.

[192] 1 Corinthians 9:6,7.

[193] Malachi 3:10.

[194] Acts 5:1-12.

[195] Luke 21:1-4.

[196] Proverbs 22:9.

[197] 1 Corinthians 16:2

[198] Matthew 23:23; 1 Corinthians 9:14 suggests that it is proper for clergy to be paid from what the members contribute.

[199] Richard J. Foster, *The Challenge of the Disciplined Life* (San Francisco, CA: HarperCollins, 1998), p. 72.

[200] *Ibid.*, p. 71.

[201] James 2:17.

202 Henri J. Nouwen, *Bread for the Journey: Reflections for Every Day of the Year* (London: Darton, Longman & Todd, Ltd, 1996), p. 14.

203 John 3: 5-8.

204 Matthew 9:9.

205 Acts 9.

206 Alvin Plantinga,'A Christian Life Partly Lived', in: Kelly James Clark, ed., *Philosophers who Believe* (Downers Grove, Ill: InterVarsity Press, 1993), 45-82; quoted in Reinder Bruinsma, *Our Awesome God* (Boise, Id: Pacific Press Publishing Association, 2000), p.109.

207 For the classic discussion of the various titles given to Jesus, see O. Cullmann, *Christology of the New Testament* (Philadelphia: Westminster Press, 1959).

208 John 20:28.

209 John 15:15.

210 Romans 6:22.

211 Genesis 24.

212 Genesis 39:5.

213 1 Corinthians 4:2.

214 Luke 14:26.

215 Luke 14:27.

216 Matthew 8:20.

217 Romans 6:17, 18.

218 Romans 7:24.

219 Romans 6:18.

220 Deuteronomy 6:5.

221 Matthew 22:37.

222 Hebrews 5:12-14.

223 2 Peter 3:18.

224 1 Timothy 6:12; 2 Corinthians 10:4.

225 See 1 Corinthians 12.

226 Richard S. Taylor, *The Disciplined Life* (Minneapolis, Minnesota: 1962), p. 18.

227 See Luke 16:10.

228 Ephesians 2:8.

229 John 3:16.

230 *Discipleship* (New York: MacMillan Company, 1965 ed.), pp. 62, 63.

231 Matthew 19: 25, 26.

232 J. Heinrich Arnold, Discipleship – *Living for Christ in the Daily Grinds* (Farmington, PA: The Plough Publishing House, 1994), p. 35.

233 Mike Nappa, *The Courage to be a Christian*, (West Monroe, Louisiana: 2001), p. 35.

234 Timothy R. V. Foster, *101 Great Mission Statements* (London: Kogan Page, 1993), pp. 51f.

235 Matthew 28:19,20.

236 Read about it in Acts, chapter 2.

237 These statistics are collected by a number of specialized agencies. A good, annually updated, source is found in the *International Bulletin of Missionary Research* from which these statistics have been taken.

238 See Philip Jenkis, *The Next Christendom* (Oxford: Oxford University Press, 2002).

239 Acts 1:8.

240 2 Peter 3:18.